W9-AZI-392

True Life in God

Vassula

Volume Ten
(Notebook 87 - Notebook 94)

Original Handwriting Edition

Published by

Trinitas™

Declaration

The decree of the Congregation for the Doctrine of the Faith, A.A.S. 58, 1186 (approved by Pope Paul VI on October 14, 1966) states that the Nihil Obstat and Imprimatur are no longer required on publications that deal with private revelations, provided they contain nothing contrary to faith and morals.

The publisher wishes to manifest unconditional submission to the final and official judgment of the Magisterium of the Church.

True Life in God
Vassula
Volume Ten (Notebook 87 - Notebook 94)

Published by

Trínitas™

P.O. Box 475
Independence, Missouri, USA 64051-0475
Phone (816) 254-4489
Fax (816) 254-1469

Copyright © 1998, Vassula Ryden
ISBN: 1-883225-26-4

All rights reserved. No part of this book may be reproduced or transmitted in any form without the written permission of the author.

For further information direct all inquiries to Trinitas.

Cover photo: from Agamian Portrait, courtesy of Holy Shroud Guild. Printed in United States of America.

Also available in Spanish, French, Italian, German, Croatian, Bulgarian, Mexican, Greek, Danish, Russian, Portuguese, Japanese, and other languages. For information contact Trinitas.

Table of Contents

Other Titles Available
True Life in God

Original Handwriting Editions
My Angel, Daniel
Volume 1—NB 1-16
Volume 2—NB 17-28
Volume 3—NB 29-41
Volume 4—NB 42-53
Volume 5—NB 54-58
Volume 6—NB 59-65:35
Volume 7—NB 65:36-71:18
Volume 8—NB 71-79:28
Volume 9—NB 79-87:18

Printed Editions

Volume 1—NB 1-31
Volume 2—NB 32-58
Volume 3—NB 59-63
Volume 4—NB 64-71
Volume 5—NB 71-79
Volume 6—NB 79-84:17
Volume 7—NB 84:18-94

Books Related to the Messages
When God Gives a Sign—Laurentin
Insights into TLIG—Four authors
Vassula and the CDF—O'Connor

By Father Michael O'Carroll:
Vassula of the Sacred Heart's Passion
Bearer of the Light
John Paul II

Books of Collected TLIG Messages
Gifts of the Holy Spirit
Prayers of Jesus and Vassula
The Ten Commandments
The Two Witnesses
Fire of Love

In Prayer
St. Michael, the Archangel

March 8, 1989 ... Here is Saint Michael:

✠ I, Saint Michael, pray without cease for this evil generation. Pray child, and obey the Lord; praise the Lord for the outpouring of His Spirit among you all.

St. Michael, thank you,

Peace to you

Photo: Courtesy of Black Rock College, Dublin, Ireland. Sculptured in Sussex Oak by Claire Sheridan.

Wisdom Educated You Through
True Life in God

Almost twelve years after our Savior began instructing His prophet, Vassula Ryden, she describes a special moment while Jesus was dictating a message to her in November 1997: "*Suddenly it was as though Jesus turned His Holy Face away and looked at the reader (the one who is reading these lines). His Face was solemn, His penetrating Eyes glued on the reader....He said*:

> **May the heart of the reader who has read these pages open! May his eyes and ears open! Up to the present time you have not grasped entirely My Heavenly Treasure, nor have you appreciated completely My gift to you. You still have not penetrated into what is beyond all price, and what I have been offering you all the days of your life.** (Notebook 92:14-16)

What is the treasure we have not entirely grasped, this gift we have yet to appreciate fully? What has He been offering us all the days of our life? Father James Fannan, P.I.M.E., Vassula's first spiritual counselor, once wrote that "*Jesus is reminding us of a fact that is often forgotten in these days: God is active in the world and united with us. ...The God who reveals Himself in these pages is above all a loving Father. ...It is very clear in these writings that if we hope to answer our Father's call of love we must have the faith of little children.*"

Jesus tells Vassula that she has responded to His bidding:

> **"to build a holy temple within you...This is why Wisdom was able to help you and through you thousands of others. Wisdom educated you and many others through this Divine Work...proof of My overflowing Love.** (NB 92:25-26)

Vassula is not only the bearer of this divine instruction but a sign of its authenticity.

> **It is My Love that leads Me now to you, generation, calling one of the most inadequate creatures amongst you, the one who lacked the knowledge not only of Scriptures but also the knowledge of My Will...to call such a wretched soul...and raise her to My Divine Heart...is a sign you should not ig-**

I

nore, it is a sign for the rest of you to grow in your confidence and learn that I call every soul to abandon its evil conduct of today and turn to Me wholeheartedly....(NB 92:28-29)

We cannot fully comprehend what is in *True Life in God*. The Holy Spirit tells Vassula: **I am filling you with My Knowledge...beyond what you can contain** (NB 93:64, NB 94:1). Indeed, those who have spent their lives studying salvation history and puzzling over eschatological mysteries recognize the enormity of what is being illuminated for us by this "Heavenly Treasure."[1] One of these scholars is Helen Tzima Otto, Ph.D., a practicing Greek Orthodox who has made it a labor of love to delve deeply into Biblical prophecy as well as the history of divine revelation in both the Orthodox and Catholic traditions over the past millennia.

In her latest book, *When Heaven Broke the Seals and Opened the Scrolls*,[2] she calls Vassula "one of the most valuable prophetic voices" in the world today. Dr. Otto finds a *"wealth of spiritual guidance directly from the Holy Ones, along with prophecies for the End Times as well as clarifications...of the book of Revelation....[Vassula's] testimony enriches, expands and elucidates much of what was still a matter of surmise, speculation, and misunderstanding...in several areas...concerning the prophecies of the End Times."* The messages, Dr. Otto believes, are evidence that *"Heaven decided to come to our rescue and provide the guidance, explanations, insights, and cross-references necessary for us to appreciate where we are standing now on the apocalyptic time line and where we are heading."*

Dr. Otto goes on to lay out considerable historical corroboration of the *True Life in God* messages. Remarking on how they have contributed to our knowledge and understanding of prophecies concerning the future of Russia, Dr. Otto believes that the specific pronouncements on Russia alone would be enough to give her *"the greatest confidence that Mrs. Ryden is a true prophetess of God...."*

Father Fernando Umana Montoya, a theologian from Colombia writes in one of his books on Vassula's charism that previous divine revelations, especially those of St. Margaret Mary Alacoque and those given at Fatima, foreshadowed the instruction in *True Life in God*. He considers that Vassula's ecumenical mission for the reunification of the Churches and the way God has given her a spiritual formation, constitute *"a genuine school of spirituality."* Father Umana declares of the messages that *"having read them carefully once, twice, three times, I am convinced Vassula is indeed one of the great prophets of today, and that her message has ecclesial and global dimensions*

II

of the first order....God wants us to be children in His arms, that we discover intimacy with Him, without which no holiness is possible."[3]

I am renowned for My Mercy and for the tenderness of My Heart; I am renowned for the weakness I have for children. (NB 92:23-24)

Father Umana asks: *"These are providential graces of the Holy Spirit for today's times. How can we close ourselves to them, how can we be blind and deaf to God's call of today to the world to save it before it is too late?"*

Today, you have heard My Voice [Through the messages of *True Life in God*—Vassula's note] and I tell you, do not waver; do not harden your hearts either, for this is My Grace passing now on you...be united to Me and rooted in Me, then no one in this world will come between you and Me. My great Return is imminent. I have come all the way to you with My Heart in My Hand...I have come to you with My Message. (NB 92:32, 34)

1. The bibliography of scholarly books and articles written by clergy and others about the *True Life in God* messages runs to seven pages. It is available from Trinitas upon request.
2. 1998, The Verenikia Press, Rock Hill, S.C. USA 29732-6589; tel.: (803) 327-9637; fax (803) 327-0467.
3. 1995 French Edition: *Vassula: An Ecumenical Charism for Our Times*, Editions Du Parvis, CH-1648 Hauteville, Switzerland.

Welcome

To the praise of Jesus and Mary

In reading the messages, read *Volume I* or *My Angel Daniel* first, then follow the books in order so that you become immersed in God's Love for you. You will understand while reading from the beginning that God is calling you to an intimate relationship with Him.

Jesus Christ asked me to tell you to always take my name, Vassula, out of the messages and replace it with your name. You will hear Him then speaking to you, re-animating your soul to move, aspire, and breathe in His Glory. God will draw you very delicately into His Heart so that you no longer belong to yourself but to the One who moves you in union with Their Oneness (The Holy Trinity).

I want to thank everyone who supports and helps to diffuse these messages. Jesus said on several occasions: "My message saves souls." Let everyone who is moved by the Holy Spirit become witnesses of God's Infinite Love. May you, too, become a disciple of these end-times.

Vassula

Publisher's Notes:

❖ Vassula uses the Jerusalem Bible for her references in the text. Occasionally there is a different chapter arrangement in the Jerusalem edition. Knowing this may help to find the references in other editions.

❖ In reading the messages and trying to live a "True Life in God," ask the Holy Spirit to be your spiritual director. Father Michael O'Carroll insists that he is only Vassula's "counselor" while the Holy Spirit is her "Director." He tells us, "This is the role the Holy Spirit will fulfill for each of us if we sincerely ask Him." Every difficulty encountered can be resolved most efficaciously through appeal to the Holy Spirit for direction.

Excerpts from Notebook 87

28 November 96 (continued from Notebook #86)...Since My Heart is the throne of grace, have confidence in My benevolence; p. 1.

✠ Know that you have a permanent place in My Sacred Heart; p. 1.

✠ Divine and irresistible is My Sacred Heart, for It holds all the riches of your salvation; p. 3.

✠ So many of My children...scorn this merciful Heart; p. 4.

✠ Happy the man who discovers the steadfastness of My Sacred Heart...beyond the price of pearls; p. 7.

✠ I have come again to revive the devotion to My Sacred Heart; p. 10.

✠ I will let this Fountain...invade this cold world, giving life wherever It will pass; p. 13.

✠ I had given...to My beloved disciple John, a glimpse of My Treasures in My Heart, that led him, in the terrors of that day, all the way to My Cross;...later on he invited Gertrude to revere My Sacred Heart...her eyes rained tears of joy; p. 14.

✠ The real knowledge is to know Us, in Our Trinitarian Holiness and live in an intimate union with Us...so let the devotion of My Sacred Heart be known to all people; p. 16.

✠ Tell them that whosoever practices this devotion...will obtain sanctifying graces...for all their household; p. 18.

4 December 96 (Las Vegas)...There are countless souls out there... who are dying...are you willing to offer Me more sacrifices to bring those souls home? p. 19.

✠ Remind them that the God they long for is always with them, blessing each one of them; p. 21.

9 December 96 (San Antonio)...The Church has neglected the devotion to My Sacred Heart; p. 23.

✠ So do not fear, all heaven is with you; there are many devout men who will help you; p. 24.

12 December 96 (Milwaukie, Oregon)...Even if your land today lies in terror because of its iniquity...be merry and rejoice for My triumph over the evil forces is near; p. 26.

✠ The calumnies and the persecutions which you bear for My sake, so generously, glorify Me...everybody in the end wears out...but your souls live forever; your achievements in My Name will not wear out and your soul will be recompensed in the end; p. 28.

20 December 96 (Back home after US tour)...The earth is rusting but My passage wears away the rust; p. 30.

✠ The Time of acute suffering is at your very doors now...those evil forces' noose is not only tightening around the Vicar of My Church but on My entire Church! p. 32.

✠ I, Jesus Christ, suffer excessive torments to watch the criminal slaughter of innocent babies, human sacrifices; p. 35.

✠ I...am pouring My blessings on him who perseveres in holiness and does not succumb in disgrace; p. 36.

✠ If they do not recognize the mighty works I am doing through your nothingness, pray for them that I lift the veil from their eyes; p. 39.

24 December 96...I will be sending you for this journey a brother; p. 43.

29 December 96...What have you done, My child! *p. 45.*

✠ Remind everyone what the beauty of My Spirit brings to mankind; it brings them peace, love, gentleness, kindness, patience, truthfulness, generosity, self-control and mercy which will lead them into eternal life; p. 48.

✠ If you are by far My most tormented messenger of your times, it is because you come from Me, and the Word that is given to you is true; p. 49.

7 January 97...I have given you this grace to call Me and be in My company; p. 50.

✠ I and you will continue restoring My House; p. 52.

13 January 97 (Manila)...Allow My Hand to reveal greater things still,... allow My Voice to be heard so that I sanctify My people with Instruction; p. 53.

even to the most wretched among you;
My Heart is active because I am the
Word and the Word of God is something alive and active; My Heart is
invulnerable in Its Glory; It is bene-
volent and full of mercy when you are
in need of help; since My Heart is
the throne of grace, have confidence in
My benevolence, I sympathize with your
ignorance, do not lose courage; know
that you have a permanent place in
My Sacred Heart; I am the Word of God

2

and from My Mouth comes an incisive sword; I am here, and My Heart will undertake all things that are not right and put them right with My sword; My Sacred Heart is not complicated, I am not a complicated God, because I am like a lamp, shining from within and from without, and completely lucid, therefore, you will never be misled, and I will reassure you all the time that holiness will be rewarded in the end; My Sacred Heart is so lucid and pure, It is the Light of

3

the world; divine and irresistible is
My Sacred Heart, for It holds all the riches
of your salvation; it is he who receives
this Heart graciously, that will be
acknowleding Us as thrice Holy, with
reverence, faithfulness and honour,
    and in My divinity I will lead him
into eternal life ♡ My Sacred Heart,
throbs with love for mankind because
It is loving to man; if you approach Me
like a child, I will place My Sacred
Heart in the palm of your hand and

when you will see My Treasures, with
learned sayings revealing My mysteries
and My secrets, your 'holy' fear for
Me will seize you because you will realize that I am God, triune but
One in the unity of essence, dearer to
you than all 'the' wealth of the
world and even your own life;
ah Vassula.... mercy is to be found with
Me, yet so many of My children abandon
and scorn this merciful Heart; exile
though you are on earth, creation,

5

open your eyes to contemplate My
Sacred Heart, open your eyes and
your heart to the marvels engraved
in My Heart; I will not hide My
inestimable Treasures from you; although
you are an exile, I shall open
the door of My Heart and when your
eyes will contemplate in your misery
the majesty of My Heart, your soul
will be overcome with an incessant
longing for My rulings, and My decrees
will become your delight and your

6

counsellors; then you will voluntarily ask Me to become the victim of the Victim, the crucifix of the Crucified and you will proclaim My decrees to the world, without fear of disgrace, remembering Who had found you, an exile, in the exile ♡; then you will say to Me, showing Me My Sacred Heart: "Master, here I will stay for ever, this is the home I have chosen ♡" faithfulness is the essence of My Word, and I am known to

7

be faithful and true; there is no deceit in My Heart; My Sacred Heart _is_ your heaven, filled with righteous rulings; happy the man who discovers the steadfastness of My Sacred Heart which is beyond the price of pearls; nothing you could covet is its equal;

My sons, My daughters, there is nothing equal to My Sacred Heart, for I am the Alpha and the Omega; and the ways of My Sacred Heart are delightful ways, leading into the

8

intimacy so desired by Us* ; to what can you compare My Sacred Heart ? to a Fountain that makes the gardens fertile ? yes, so if any man is thirsty, let him come to Me ! let the man come and drink; My Heart is a well of living water ; come and immerse yourself in those streams* that flow out from My Sacred Heart ; My Sacred Heart is your guarantor and the Tree of Life for those who will possess It ♡

*¹ | The Trinity.

*² / Jesus was speaking about His Spirit.

9

do not let your feet take you down to death; learn that My tender Sacred Heart is glorious and majestic, dependable, faithful and true; It is framed in steadfastness, transcending the heavens; It raises, Vassula, the poor from dust * and out of their misery, to give them a place in Its depths, in the depths of Infinite Mercy; let My Sacred Heart be the Root that supports you and you, you have been grafted on to Me

* Jesus was hinting this for me; the way He raised me & gave me a place in His Heart;

10

to share My rich sap that provides you
with life, eternal life; so remain
grafted on Me to be part of Me and
your life will be spared; Vassula,
I have come again to revive the devotion
to My Sacred Heart, happy all those
who follow this devotion; the world,
is dead to love because it has distanced
itself from Us,* and by forsaking
the Fountain of Wisdom, it died in
its drought; this is why I have
come, with My Heart in My Hand, to

* The Trinity

11

you so you feel the pulsations of My Heart;
do not be surprised, have you not read
that a Fountain will spring from the
House of Yahweh *¹? and like cascades
this living water *² will pour out of My
Heart.... yes, so that all of you
gain freedom, this freedom that is solely found in My Spirit ♡ I have
come to you, not because of your merits,
since you had none, I have not only
chosen you because of your wretchedness

*¹ Joel 4:18   *² Holy Spirit

12

and your nothingness, as you tell people,
but it was also because of your in-
significance and your total ignorance
in all matters that concerned My Sacred
Heart, yes! * and My Church too;
drenched in sin and not virtue, portrait of your society and far from My
Own traits, you were appalling even
in My Angels' eyes! yet, I have come
to you, puny little creature, to show
the world the Power of My Sacred

* I thought, of the Church too...

13

Heart and My Infinite Mercy; I have
come in your ignorance and charged
you with a task far beyond your
means and I have made My Sacred
Heart known to you and I will
continue to make It known in this
cold world drenched in its blood from
its crimes; I will let this Fountain*
from My Sacred Heart invade this cold
world, giving life wherever It will pass
and My Promise will be accomplished
because My Holy Spirit, the Giver of

* Jesus speaks about His Holy Spirit

14

life will govern this wicked society and turn it into an upright people; then holiness and justice will be their consort; Vassula, I had given, in the past, to My beloved disciple John, a glimpse of My Treasures in My Heart, that led him, in the terrors of that day, all the way to My Cross; then, later on, he invited Gertrude to revere My Sacred Heart, showing her the value of the Treasures hidden in My Heart; her eyes rained tears of joy when she

15

saw those divine Treasures; I have been longing to reveal to you in your day and age the Riches of a 'mystery' kept secret for endless ages; so honour My Sacred Heart and be innocent, be the salt of the earth and the light, so that you will shine in the world like a bright star, because you will be offering it * the Word of Life; fall on your knees now and praise Me! see how mighty are My wonders? see how great

*   the world

16

are My marvels? let My Yoke be light on you and not burden you and you will have no trace of fatigue .... pursue the path I have traced for you and tell My people that no one can survive with his intellect only, and I never reveal Myself to those who claim to have knowledge only of earthly things, for this is not the real knowledge that comes from God; the real knowledge is to know Us, in Our Trinitarian Holiness and live in an intimate

17

union with Us; I have no favourites,
so let the devotion of My Sacred Heart
be known to all people*; be one in
Us; We love you, dear child ♡ receive
Our blessings;   ΙΧΘΥΣ ⊰⊱◦

Later:

yes! this* was given to you on the eleventh
anniversary of My saving Message; I will
continue to fill your mouth and nourish
you with My Word; you will continue
to obtain from My Heart abundant

[1] * Jesus means not only to Catholics but all others too.
[2] * The Message above.

18

sanctifying graces to accomplish your mission; and as I said to My other apostles of My Sacred Heart, I also tell you: love this Heart that is so unloved, revive My devotion of My Sacred Heart and tell 'them'* that whosoever practices this devotion, they will obtain sanctifying graces not only for themselves but also for all their house- hold;" and you, My loved one, be one with Me; ♡ ic

* To the people

19
Las Vegas.   4. 12. 96

My Lord, I love you.

ah Vassula, I invite you to take your rest in My Sacred Heart; come, child of My Father, come, I am your God, I am your Rock, your portion; the one and only who raised you up with Wisdom for My Glory; it is I who guided you with tenderness and counselled you with My Heart ....
ah Vassula,* there are countless souls

* Jesus sighed

20

out there in the world who are
dying and My Heart pains Me and
I am distraught at the sight of these
dying souls ... * Vassula, are you willing
to offer Me more sacrifices to bring
those souls home? yes, in My Sacred
Heart? - yes Lord ....

put then your trust in Me; do not
weary working for Me and with Me;
be effaced so that My Spirit guides
you where I want you to go;

* Jesus paused for a while before asking His
question.

21

proclaim My Name with praise to
all the nations I am sending you
with the power of My Holy Spirit;
do not let go of My Hand; allow
Me to keep your hand in Mine;
come, your Faithful God is with you
in His Faithful Love ♡ I bless you
dear soul; go now and join in
their prayers and remind them that
the God they long for is always
with them, blessing each one of
them; dwell in My Sacred Heart

22

forever and pray for the conversion of souls and be constant in your faithfulness as I am Faithful ♡ ic

U.S.A.   9. 12. 96

be in peace. tell your counsellor :
" I am filled with joy that at last your thoughts on My Sacred Heart are blossoming in your mouth* ; I know that you always considered

---

* Fr. O'Carroll spoke of the Treasures of the Sacred Heart that are reserved for our times.

23

My Heart a Heaven, but had not so many opportunities to expose My Heart <u>as now</u>; *[1] the Church has neglected the devotion to My Sacred Heart; at one time it was good of you to share with Me in My sorrows and My grief *[2]; I value the interest that is mounting up in you to glorify My Heart; I self - suffice as you know, but I have chosen you

*[1] Jesus gives those opportunities when we travel to conferences where people listen.

*[2] At Cap de la Madeleine. Fr. O'Carroll had an experience.

24

and My Vassula to offer the world all that you can to attract them to receive this Heart that loves them; your *¹ sacrifices are pleasing to Me and I will see to it that I will fulfill all your needs out of the Riches of My Heart; I have, as you noticed given you My three angels *² to escort you; yes .... including My three Archangels; so do not fear, all heaven is

*¹ Fr. O'Carroll and I.
*² That is : Bob, Pat and Tom.

25

with you ; there are many devout men
who will help you ; be fearless , I
am with you ;   ic

U. S. A. 12. 12. 96

Lord, let me cling on You,
   so that You may come to
     my rescue;

I love You and I thank You,
   giving You praise
for allowing me to know
     Your Name so that
I too may be protected;

In Your great love, You
answer me every time I invoke
    Your Name ;

God, You are greatly to be
   feared because of Your Power

26

May You show Your kindness
to me when I am in
trouble; let Your smile
be on me to show
to the nations that You are
with me;

peace be with you; in My Name, speak
and do not be afraid; put your
trust in Me; My majesty covers the
heavens, and even if your land today
lies in terror because of its iniquity,
My majesty and My brightness will
cover your land* and every evil

* The Triumph of the Lord.

27

shall be revealed since now evil hides
in the darkness of the earth; do
not fear; be merry and rejoice for
My triumph over the evil forces is
near; so, go, My daughter and
do not refrain from speaking when
it will do good; gain souls for Me,
be My net; let Me cast you out
again; do all you can and I will do
the rest; vow to remain faithful to Me and serve Me in a spirit
of piety and fortitude; I shall

28

never fail you and will refuse you
nothing that would bring the sinners
to conversion and a change of heart;
you will find, therefore, before you,
My protection; the calumnies and
the persecutions which you bear for
My sake, so generously, glorify Me;
the way people treat you with
wickedness and spite and which you
bear in silence for the sake of
Me your Saviour, touches Me to tears;
everybody in the end wears out, just

29

as clothes wear out, but your souls live forever; your achievements in My Name will not wear out and your soul will be recompensed in the end; do not lose My Peace and may you remain strong, always grasping Wisdom's teachings; have now a happy heart and fill it with the joy I have in My Heart, filled by all those who desire Me, your God;

A ☧ Ω

30

20. 12. 96

Back home after many conferences or prayer meetings done in the USA.

♡ I give you My Peace, My child; persevere in justice and virtue; look at My triumphs, count the score! * the earth is rusting but My passage wears away the rust; this is why I have put zeal in you for My House, so that I and you work together to devour the rust that is like a layer

* Twenty - three prayer meetings where I spoke in twenty - eight days, all over the States, with many people including priests attending,

31

of crust on My people's hearts; I intend, with My passage, to take away that crust and leave their hearts shining with My glory, and while My Word is being unfolded to them, My Light will bring them light ♡ ah, Vassula, I have directed your steps into My Path, as I had promised you, so do not be afraid, I am with you and no evil can win any power over you. if I had chosen to send you in this

32

vast nation,*[1] so intensively to remind My people of their real foundation and that the Glory descends only from above, it is because the Time is near, the Time of acute suffering is at your very doors now .... those evil forces' noose is not only tightening around the Vicar of My Church, but on My entire Church! no, you have not spent yourselves in vain for[*2]

*[1] The U.S.A.   *[2] Fr. O'Carroll and I.

33

have revealed My Glory in many hearts
and I have reminded My people of
the power that I wield by giving
them many graces; therefore My child,
I am victorious ♡ My work, through
you, is done and I fill it with
My splendour and My majesty; this
I do to remind My people of My
Power, My Mercy, My Tenderness and
My Love; there will be more riches
and wealth revealed to you in
these coming days, from My Sacred

34

Heart .... and you, My daughter, let royal dignity be yours in the hours of persecution, so that you may glorify Me; all that you bear for My sake, touches Me; bear for Me, My loved one and console Me in this way .... devote yourself entirely, body and soul to the service of My Church and to the service of your brothers and sisters, offer these sacrifices for their benefit; endure those brief pains and trials for My sake, by

35

remembering that under the very skies you are living, in the hours of the night, I, Jesus Christ, suffer excessive torments to watch the criminal slaughter of innocent babies, human sacrifices perpetrated with blasphemy against My Name*, and for the downfall of the present papacy; I tell you, whatever you spend as sacrifice, My Arm will uphold you, so that you continue to spread My

* I understood 'Church' too.

36

Messages far and wide, while the hands of the blasphemers are stretched out so infamously against My Holy Sacrifice, My House and My Word, I, for My part, am pouring My blessings on him who perseveres in holiness and does not succumb in disgrace; I will entice many hearts to become like sacred vessels carrying My Word; yes? *

Lord, You are showing me how

* He knew I wanted to say something.

37

Your Power works, and You make
no secrets of Your Plans, but to
someone as weak as myself, born
of sin, how am I to understand
the boasts of my persecutors?

The hour of darkness is here; how
and where am I to "hang in there?"

this is My own lament too; A lament
on the hardening of their heart .... a
veil of shadow hangs on their eyelids,
daughter, their hearts harbour no
peace and their trophy is called :
lack - of - love .... but your King
is in your favour; nevertheless, there

38

are other powers behind, those
whom* I mentioned; these powers do
not come from Me; you see, Vassula,
I am, through these Messages, parading
their assassin plans on My Church, I
am parading their deceitfull designs to
the world; this is why many of them
want to wall in My Words given to
you in these Messages;

* Jesus is making a distinct difference
   between a regular persecutor whose heart
has hardened and the 'other powers' which origi-
nate from Darkness; in other words; 'evil forces.'

39

But I am a poor wretch
and no champion of defence.
I am descriminated and
treated unjustly.

may you be blessed all the days of
your life for this alone! although both
sorts of persecutors*[1] are looting your
honour and your honesty you have
become My Canticle; if they*[2] do not
recognize the mighty works I am doing
through your nothingness, pray for

*[1] The regular ones with hearts of stone and
the powers of darkness.
*[2] The ones with a hardened heart.

40

them that I lift the veil from their
eyes .... I will complete your journey with
you and I will continue to be your
rod, your lamp and your drink;
do not be afraid when you are
attacked, you will have great strength
if you fear Me and honour Me
and if you will do what is pleasing
to Me; I, Myself, will prepare
what you need for this journey and
We, the Two Hearts*, will march

* The Sacred Heart and the Immaculate Heart
of Mary.

41

together with you, infuriating on our
journey the mobs of evil powers as
we walk by them, becoming a
menace to them while we advance;
we will storm their city of evils and
these evil forces will have to face
Me, your God, in all My Divinity *;
today they are raging like wild
beasts because they know that Our

* Because that is exactly what these
  evil forces are aiming at: Christ's
           Divinity.   They want to deny
  the Divinity of Christ and His Glorious
  Resurrection.

42

Triumph *¹ is soon to come; put your trust in Me and be like a loud book; I have more to say, but for today this is enough for you;

I love you, dear soul, and I bless you; ic

24. 12. 96

(I had a long journey to go but fr. O' Carroll decided to stop travelling with me. I was wondering if I was supposed to go alone...)

Lord ?

I Am; you are not to go on your own; *²

*¹ Triumph of the Two Hearts
*² This came like a command.

43

I will be sending you for this journey a
brother*[1]; he will be your companion in
those meetings; I know how anxious he is
to help in these difficult times, this is
why I am sending him to you; do not
allow your heart to be troubled by those
who persecute you, nor by those*[2] who follow
illusory errands; they are supplying their
own needs, not Mine ... they are carried
along by every wind that comes their way;

*[1] That was Fr. James Fannan who "happened"
to be in Rome and was free all that month.
He had come from Bangladesh.

*[2] He made me understand whom He was talking about.

44

these are the ones that deepen My Wounds; and so, My beloved, I am sending this brother to you precisely for this journey; may what you do for My Sacred Heart bring many back to Us to share Our Eternal Glory; I, Jesus, bless you; ic;

29.12.96

My Lord?

I Am; before you I stand; fear not My child;* have you not heard that

* His Presence was not only glorious and majestic but had also all the splendour of His Divinity, which made me stagger.

45

obedience to God comes before obedience to men? <u>what have you done, My child!</u> *

(When I heard this last sentence, "I felt God's surprise but I felt at the same time that He was 'shocked', and His reproach was as this of a mother who surprises her child in doing something wrong. There was no harshness at all, there was also dis-appointment and sadness. — While He was uttering these few words, He made me understand that He uttered them before; and before He completed the sentence, He gave me a light of perception of where & to whom He had given these words. After the message was comple-ted, I opened Gn. 4:10 and read word for word when →

* Although in the previous message God made it clear to me that I was not to travel on my own in that very long trip, I was influenced by fr. O'Carroll saying that I could travel by myself and by a friend who said that tickets would be cheaper if I met Fr. Fannan in Indonesia, instead of Fr. Fannan travel-ling from Switzerland with me. Because of this I had consented ....

46

He had surprised Cain walking alone in the open country after he had killed his brother Abel. — Just by that, I realized how grave my sin was ...)

♡ you belong to Me and although you are a nothing My Love will always sustain you, although you are wretched, My Mercy will always bring you to your inheritance; yes, it will bring you into My Sacred Heart; you are worth nothing in front of My glory and before My Saints,*

* I was glad to hear these words so that everybody reads them especially those who never cease putting me on a high pedestal saying, "Vassula, Vassula," instead of "God, God, praise be to God!"

47

yet when you are in My bosom, you are hidden in Me, you are in the One who justifies sinners*¹, then your soul, puny little creature, is considered as justified because of Me; this was one of your falls, but however grave your sin was*², grace now will be even greater since you have realized*³ what you have done, and you have come to Me to ask My forgiveness; now you are alive again, not by your own power but by My

*¹ Forgives us.
*² the sin of disobedience. *³ While writing this, He asked me to add " not on your own, but by My Grace "...

48

Power; ♡ come to Me always before you take any decision and consult Me, I will always give you good counsel and I will always respond to your needs; observe My commandment to you and do not grieve Me; remind everyone what the beauty of My Spirit brings to mankind; it* brings them peace, love, gentleness, kindness, patience, truthfulness, generosity, self-control and mercy which will lead them into eternal

* The beauty of the Spirit

49

life ♡ never tire, My child, of working for ♡Me, and although your crosses are many, do not complain; — if you are by far My most tormented messenger of your times, it is because you come from Me, and the Word that is given to you is true; My Word gives evidence that this generation's ways are evil and binding to the underworld, but I will remain with you, and My Holy Spirit will be your Guardian and your Lamp, your Joy and your Strength; He will

50

keep you cheerful since you are hidden in Us who are thrice Holy; come to Me in complete confidence and remember: your trials are My Glory ic

" Yahweh is tender and compassionate,
slow to anger, most loving;
his indignation does not last for ever,
his resentment exists a short time only;
he never treats us, never punishes us,
as our guilt and our sins deserve. "
(Ps. 103, 8-10)

7. 1. 97

Lord ?

I Am; I have given you this grace to

51

call Me and be in My company; so now I give you My Peace; these moments delight Me; be prudent and lean on Me; — tell Me, little one, are you happy to be with Me as you are now?

How can I not be? Yahweh is on my side and He is good to me. You are on my side, so I fear nothing.
The Holy Spirit is on my side like a brilliant sun and is my guide and safety.
I extol You, my God, I give thanks to You, for all the good You do to me.

happy are you who received this gift

52

from the Father, it set you free and
all your household; it set many
people free .... allow Me now to rest
in you, and you, come, My beloved,
and rest in Me; let nothing harm
you, let nothing take away your peace
and your joy ; if I say ' your ',
it is because I have offered you My
Peace as a gift and My Joy too; keep
them, treasure them and safeguard
them; come, I and you will continue
restoring My House; be prudent;

53

I will guard you; we, us? I am
never away from you; God-is-with-
you, and I bless you;

Manila   13 . 1 . 97

never doubt of My faithfulness; peace
be with you; I am never away from
you; your Creator is your Lamp, so
do not fear in this darkness;
   created in My Love for this Love
Message, I bless you; Vassula, I,
Jesus, am pleased with your work ....
allow My Hand to reveal greater things

54

still, for this I ask you to remain faithful to Me; allow My Voice to be heard so that I sanctify My people with Instruction; I have proved My Love to you, Vassula, My chosen one, by revealing to you the tenderness of My Sacred Heart; all I ask from you now is a return of love: love for Love, heart for Heart; I bless you in My tenderness; go in peace and carry My Word; ic

Excerpts from Notebook 88

26 January 97...*I am your divine Spouse who opened your ear to hear My sweet conversation and kindled a desire in you like a flame; p. 8.*

✠ A heart founded on prayer, love and humility will not flinch at the critical moment of temptation, but will chase the demons away; p. 9.

✠ We would go in the gardens of My Heart and our friendship would be such that even My angels would desire your place; p. 11.

✠ I am the sole Heart with this one of your Mother who are perfect and unique in Our Love and Fidelity; p. 17.

✠ Allow Me to integrate you into My Body in which you can have a peaceful retreat with me; I will take you by your hand and draw you into the chamber of My Heart; p. 18.

✠ It is the Heart of complete Unity, who does not differentiate you from one another, since you all belong to this Heart; p. 22.

✠ Set your heart into My Heart, so that one day I can truly say to you: "come, My child, come and share My Throne with Me; p. 24.

28 January 97...*I will come, daughter, in My Lordly style and in My magnificence to overthrow the proud of heart; p. 30.*

✠ Your mouth ceaselessly proclaimed the Truth in all My assemblies; p. 32.

✠ By lending Me your ear just a little, you received Wisdom's sayings so that I, the Lord, may be remembered in My Mercy by all of you; p. 33.

✠ From this frailty My Word will be heard saying to all the nations: 'God is near you,' p. 34.

✠ I would hide none of My secrets from you; My Hands in which you placed your heart are sensitive and compassionate, My beloved, so do not fear; p. 37.

✠ I have given you a pair of hands...I have blessed them so that they do not weary of writing and remain bound to Mine for all eternity; p. 38.

NB
88

✠ What can I give in return to you, My chosen one, for all the miles you have made for Me, and for all the hours your feet stood, for My sake, in My assemblies? p. 39.

✠ Approach Me you who desire Me and replenish yourself from Me; I will offer you this retreat and this pilgrimage in the gardens of My Body; p. 41.

✠ From My Feet obtain strength so that your own will not feel any burden heavy to carry; p. 43.

✠ In this pilgrimage, My loved one will cry out to My angels and to My saints: "how right it is to love Him!" p. 44.

✠ Vassula to Jesus: "What will my own Orthodox people say to all of this!...They are not used to such talk!" [Jesus responds:] They will get used to it as soon as their soul goes to heaven; p. 45.

✠ I want to train you spiritually in My Body, and to make you strong to love sincerely and learn self-control; I am like a mother feeding and looking after her own children; p. 46.

✠ I made you responsible for delivering My Love Hymn to all nations and you still have a long way to go; p. 47.

✠ My Hands have done many good works that are not recorded in The Book; no king has ever been known to have served his subordinates as I, who am the King of kings, served; p. 49.

✠ You will learn in this pilgrimage of My Hands how I served faithfully and performed works that no one has ever done; p. 51.

✠ I will take you in the garden of My Mouth, there you will have your pilgrimage, how distraught I could be when your mouths who receive Me, infect your spirit and your soul by poisonous words on one another; p. 54.

✠ Let your eldest Brother now carry you to have your pilgrimage in His Eyes so that your soul may contemplate the perfect light, the principle lamp of the body; p. 59.

✠ Do not allow your eyes rest on any misconduct but lift them to heaven; p. 61.

7

Publisher's Notice

Vassula is withholding for the present
time publication of the following messages:
NB 87—pages 55, 56, 57, 58, 59, 60, 61, 62, 63,
and 64; NB 88—pages 1, 2, 3, 4, 5, 6, and 7.

26 . 1 . 97

Lord, I love Your Sacred Heart
   which floods me with Its Love;
Yes, like a flowing water is
   the Heart of my King;
and now, my King says to me:

8

" Why have you kept me waiting
for so long ? The flowers are
already approaching on earth ; daughter
so longed for, come to Me ! come
to taste the sweetness of My Heart ! "

I am your divine Spouse who opened your
ear to hear My sweet conversation and
kindled a desire in you like a flame, I
stepped into your life to reveal My
beauty to you so that your soul succumbs to My charms ; I came to prepare your
heart, waking up your love so that you
drink from the Source of My Heart which
is sweeter than wine ; then, you would seek

9

My resplendant perfection and offer yourself voluntarily to Me; then I, I for
My part, would celebrate My Strength
and My Glory for having overpowered you*;
ah, daughter-of-the-King*², I had called
you before My angels so that you and
your generation tastes My Love; and now,
dearest one, who constantly trembles for
fear of being deceived, your Lord, Father
and God of your life, tells you: do
not fear, for a heart founded on prayer,

* It means the evil in me.
*² Vassiliki means also ' daughter of the King.

10

love and humility will not flinch at
the critical moment of temptation, but
will chase the demons away; have you
not noticed how I have 'exhaled 'a
perfume like incense on you to attract your
'attention? and now 'that you are
with Me let Me ask you: do 'you know
what My Sacred Heart' desires*? that you come
to Me as a lily so that I enjoy your heart
once I engulf it entirely into My Own
Sacred Heart, love for 'Love, 'heart for

* I could not guess.

II

Heart; come, just like an ocean swallows up a drop of water, so do I want you to disappear in Me; I love you to folly and I would like to take you into the nuptial chamber of My Heart, solely for Me, just I and you, so that together we can share a retreat, or is it a pilgrimage you want? is this *¹ what you want ? *²

we would go in the gardens of My Heart and our friendship would be such that even My angels would desire your place;

*¹ It means the Latter. *² I sighed not knowing what my Lord wants and means.

12

ah, if only you knew, My beloved one, the love I have for you .... whatever you choose, pilgrimage or retreat, you would not have to walk, I will carry you in My embrace and relieve your feet which stood for Me* during hours in your mission, ministering for Me; does not dew relieve the heat? in the same way I will relieve your feet; Vassula, have you understood why I have come to you as the Sacred Heart? I have come in this way so that, from this very

* Jesus said this ending with a tone of emotion; He slightly shook His divine Head.

13

Heart,* you obtain Mercy .... yes, not just you, but all of you; come now; why the trembling? have I not espoused you to Myself with a ring? have I not given you a glimpse on the delights of My Heart? have I not shown you the goodness of My Heart? so why this hesitation?

Lord, I simply do not comprehend a
    bit of what Your wishes are,
this offer that You want to perform
    with me, this pilgrimage or retreat.
I do not understand.

My beloved, whom I raised and called

* Jesus was showing with His forefinger His Heart.

14

for Myself and for My Glory, come now
and feast in Me; I will be your joy
and your smile, I will be your banquet,
I will let you profit from the Treasures
of My Heart; take a look at Me, take
a look at My Heart .... look, have
I not opened the gate of My Heart for
you? My Royal Heart was offered to
you; come and find your joy in Me;
if the world has sworn to hurt
you, I in My turn have sworn to
protect you from absorbing their poison,

15

and designate you for My Glory; if the
world is treacherous, it was to prove
to you, that I alone am always
faithful in My love and in My friendship; therefore, you whom I nurtured,
to you I say: do not get discouraged
with what has happened to you; I
have allowed this weight to overwhelm
you for My greatest glory; I am, My dearest
love, ready now to do just about any
thing for your spiritual growth and
the sanctification of your soul; your

16

company with Me will be complete,
and I will feel more free to transport
you in My Arms; I will be more free
to run away with you and strengthen
our union; I have told you once that
even your closest friends would not understand you and they would cause you
impressive wounds, and that by doing so,
you would become the victim of their
thought but that they too would
become the victims of their own
fault; I may still reward them

17

afterwards for all the good things they had done and I will not forget their sacrifices but I will reprimand them heavily for their harshness towards My chosen one, their lack of charity and gentleness .... you will never find in this world, My dove, the perfect heart, no, it is non-existent; I am the sole Heart with this one of your Mother who are perfect and unique in Our Love and Fidelity ♡ come to Me so that I give you ♡ the gift of My

18

Love; I have stored so many other gifts for you, My beloved; come to your Spouse, and allow Me to integrate you into My Body in which you can have a peaceful retreat with Me; I will take you by your hand and draw you into the chamber of My Heart where we will embrace in our love; in My Love I will restore and console your soul, with kisses of My mouth*; I will

* Sg 1:1

19

restore you, strengthing your love;
and you, in this love, even though
it is imperfect, you will console your
Consoler, by becoming a balm to My
Wounds; and while I, your King,
will be resting in your arms, savour-
ing every drop of your love, I
will be showing you now and
then, My sister, My Royal Heart,
this Heart that raised you up in Our *
Courts, this Heart that is All; this
Heart that gives itself abundantly to

* The Holy Trinity

20

all mankind; this Heart that composed musical melodies and songs for His loved ones; yes, the One who sings to you now is the Lover of mankind, the Spouse of the whole earth*; while some of you have no memory of your God, to this day, I, in My Faithfulness and in the greatness of My Love, come to you to offer you My Heart, greater offer than this, one I cannot give; let your eyes then marvel at the

allusion to Is. 54 : 5

21

beauty of My Heart; it is the Heart
of the great Sacrifice; it is the Heart
of the New Covenant; it is the
Heart of the True Vine, it is the
Heart nearest to the Father's Heart;
it is the Heart that shines in the
dark, and that darkness could never
overpower; it is the Heart of the
World made flesh and who lived
among you; it is the Heart that
lives in your heart so that all of
you become the heart of My Heart;

22

and the heart of Our Heart; it is the Heart of the martyrs and the prophets, who wholeheartedly did the Will of the Father and glorified Him by their perseverance, their docility and their perfect obedience ♡ it is the Heart of complete Unity, who does not differentiate you from one another, since you all belong to this Heart; it is the Heart who prayed to the Father that you may all be one is Us ♡ ....

what is the Heart of the ♡ Lord

23

like? the Heart of the Lord is like an infinite ocean of Love and Mercy; it is like an incomparable and inestimable treasure, that whosoever holds it, will never let go, knowing that in it is eternal life ♡ My Heart is like a blazing furnace of ♡ Love, ready to consume your heart in its Love; My Heart is Light, outshining all the constellations put together; time slips by between dawn and dusk and all things pass swiftly, but My Love is constant

24

and forever; come all you who thirst,
but do not even know it; come and
acknowledge this Heart of your God, so
that you may understand Me and
know Me as thrice Holy; come and
possess this Heart so that you set your
hearts on My Kingdom and all that is
righteous; come and set your heart
into My Heart, so that one day I
can truly say to you:" come, My
child, come and share My Throne
with Me;

25

I have always known you, My own, My remnant; bone of My Bone, flesh of My Flesh, come, part of Me; come and inherit what was yours since the foundations of the earth; breath of My Breath, you belong to the One who moves you in intimate union in Our Oneness ♡ ah fruit - of - My - Heart, this is what I would be showing you, while I would be reposing, like a contented child, in your embrace; promise Me, My Vassula, My loved one, to let your

26

Bridegroom, repose undisturbed in your
heart *; learn from your Beloved:
     I am gentle and humble in Heart,
and in Me your soul will always find
its rest; let Me find the same in you,
let Me find gentleness and humility;

'I do not want to stir my Love, nor rouse
it, until it please to awake!' (Sg.2:7)
therefore, teach me to be as You want
     me to be so that I may be pleasing
to You.

* I understood that, if I lacked peace in
   my heart, I would disturb the silence
        My Saviour would like to find.

27

My sweetness felt in your heart will be the reminder of My Holy Presence reposing in your heart ♡ but remember also that you need only say : " I am slipping, " and My Love, immediately will support you, lavishing you with thousands of consolations, My beloved; I bless you, giving you My kiss of Love; I, Jesus Christ, am always with you; we, us? ic

28

28. 1 . 97

_____ O Lord, give me Your Strength
to proclaim Your Word with fervour,
So many are waiting anxiously to
hear Your Loving Word and listen in
silence and in thirst;

Let Your Words drop on them,
        one by one to refresh them,
Look how they are in Your assemblies,
    open-mouthed, as if to catch the
year's last showers;
    For the sake of Your great Love,
let Your rain fall on lands where no
    one lives and make out of a
    sterile land, gardens; give drink to
the lonely wastes, making grass spring
where everything was dry;

    Come, in Your Lordly style, and
drive frantic the proud of heart;
come and pull down, with Your Royal
Sceptre, the haughty from their thrones and
exalt the lowly, the meek;

29

then toss me out in the tempest,
for my confidence in You is complete;
and my hope of safety as well;
I fear no harm, beside me Your
    Lordly Presence is there, singing ballads
to me about Your Triumphs; and while You are
laughing, Your laughter sounding like running streams,
You lift me on Your Wings to ride the skies and
be alone with You so that You whisper
to me the secrets of Wisdom;

My Guardian and my Delight,
    You give me more joy to my heart
than others ever knew, for all the
    treasures and kingdoms of the world

    Joy of my heart, show us all
the light of Your Holy Face!

daughter, I give you My blessings and
My peace; I will do marvelous

30

things, for I will draw water from
the springs of My Heart; and your feverish
faces will be refreshed; I will be your
shade from the heat of this tempest
you are in; I will come, daughter, in
My Lordly style and in My magnificence to overthrow the proud of Heart;
and because I have set My throne in
you, daughter, you shall not be
mangled in this tempest; your
Loved One will carry you on His
Wings to ride the skies while pouring

31

on you, like rain, words of Wisdom
from My Heart *; and now your Guardian
and your delight asks you to lean on
His Heart .... ah, My beloved, what
makes you run away from My invitation? I am your Maker and I have

---

* I saw our Lord and King, while we were riding the
skies,   sitting side by side with me, that He
leaned towards me and covered my head with the
most beautiful veil of white lace, which in its
whiteness was shimmering as though it had
    diamonds on it. He closed the veil
on me so that only my face was seen.
I understood that the veil symbolized
    His Words of Wisdom, that He was pouring
on me, covering me entirely.

32

the right to invite* you to rest in Me
after your labours? your mouth
ceaselessly proclaimed the Truth in all My
assemblies, and from your lips came praise
and honour for Me, your God; your eyes
never turned away from My Presence, but
observed My ways, may you be blessed
for making your Maker so happy!

then at the sound of My Name, your
ear was opened and every word coming

---

* Jesus was referring to His invitation of having a
retreat or a pilgrimage in His Body. (message of 26.1.97)
I had not really responded to that invitation.

33

from My Mouth was heard like a melody in you, like a thousand cantors chanting their hymns, so was My Word heard in your heart when you opened your ear to receive My sweetest psalms; by lending Me your ear just a little, you received Wisdom's sayings so that I, the Lord, may be remembered in My Mercy by all of you; no one could say: "He has left us in the fangs of the Enemy..." ah...then I asked you to be generous and offer Me your heart as a

34

token of your love; quick to be generous, My loved one, you gave it to Me
placing it quickly into My Divine Hands,
so that I, in My turn, fill it with
love, steadfastness and constancy; since
then, I swore to keep your heart for
Myself alone, and guard it like the
pupil of My Eye; and while My Eyes
were gazing at this frail heart, I
said : " from this frailty My Word
will be heard saying to all nations:
God is near you, He will free all

35

those who call Him; and for all those who thirst, He will give water; He will have pity on the poor and feeble and He will save the lives of many before His great Day comes;" because of your generous offering I promised to make out of your heart an exultant sacrifice; "I, her Maker and Spouse,* will sing to it My closeness so that this heart would seek only My Holy Face, and by drawing it into My Sacred

* Allusion to Is. 54:5

36

Heart, it will repulse all that is not Me, but will thirst and desire all that is Me;" your heart will be eager then to wait on Me, your God, centering all your affections you have had elsewhere, on My Royal Heart alone; yes, all your dispositions, your indispositions, your delights, your sorrows, your joys, your anguishes, your pastimes, your tears, everything, yes everything would be offered to My Heart as someone offers to the loved one,

37

a bouquet of roses; this is what I yearn for, from each one of you, from the very core of My Heart ♡ having then directed your heart in Mine, I knew that in this closeness I would find My comfort and My delight; to rejoice your soul, I would hide none of My secrets from you; My Hands in which you placed your heart are sensitive and compassionate, My beloved, so do not fear... * stretch out your hands towards

* Then looking at my hands and taking them both in His Hands, He said what followed.

38

the Sanctuary*.... I have given you a
pair of hands which I 'kissed' and
'anointed with a blessing so that they
pluck out the thorns 'encircling My
Heart; I have blessed them so
that they do not weary of writing and
remain 'bound to Mine for all 'eternity;
I have anointed them so 'that in the
end of the ceremony*², those hands will
set a 'crown of glory on My Head;

* by saying Sanctuary, I knew He was referring
   to Himself; He took both my hands and while holding them said what follows. *² By using the word 'ceremony'
                              Jesus means 'mission'

39

have you not read : " work from skilled
hands will earn its praise; "*¹ what
can I give in return to you, My chosen
one, for all the miles you have made
for Me, and for all the hours your
feet stood, for My sake, in My assemblies?

For my hunger You gave me bread *²
from Heaven, for my thirst You
offered me living water spurting from
Your Breast; You have been
gracious and loving to me, abounding
in goodness, and You have never
forsaken me. I grew in Your Courts
where You courted my soul and all
that I have obtained came from You;

*¹ Si 9: 17   *² Meaning 'spiritual manna'

40

You spoke heart to heart with me
and allowed me to possess You, and as
a lamp shining above my head You
lighted my way to show me by
which way I should go.
Blessed be You, my Lord and my God
from everlasting to everlasting;
You have provided me;
why should I then have the honour to
be given something in return of
your own deeds?

true, I have provided you with everything, but the fruits of your labours
have touched My Heart; you have
served Me voluntarily and with these
precious offerings I can only be touched;
so let Me offer you a retreat and

41

a pilgrimage in My Body....

Is this what Your Sacred Heart desires?

yes! yes .... come, you will have your
rest in My Body; forget yourself in
Me so that you take your resources
from My Feet upwards; just I and you,
approach Me you who desire Me and
replenish yourself from Me; I will offer
you this retreat and this pilgrimage
in the gardens of My Body; I will
accompany you everywhere and all
the way to My nuptial chamber

42

of My Sacred Heart where I always lead My chosen ones to exhale on them My charms like a scent of choice myrrh; while they repose their head on My Sacred Heart I refresh them from the living water from My Breast; and like concord between brothers and sisters, like a husband and wife who live happily together, we will enjoy each others' presence; * come, My loved one,

* I started to understand that Jesus wanted me to be all alone with Him for a while and this is why He did not let me book any meetings for several weeks. Jesus wants everyone to retreat in Him now and then.

43

from My Feet obtain strength so that your own will not feel any burden heavy to carry; when you walk in My foot-prints which will be your guide to follow My Principles, your going will be unhindered; when you are having your pilgrimage in My Feet, as you walk you will never set your feet on the path of the wicked nor will you walk the way that the evil go; but My Feet will lead you to avoid and turn your back on all evil,

TRUE LIFE IN GOD

44

and pass it by ; have your pilgrimage
in My Feet where they would take
you to tread on a levelled path
where all the ways are made firm ;
you will turn neither to right nor to
left, but will keep your feet clear
of evil and far from straying from
the way of Truth ; and in this
pilgrimage, My loved one will cry out
to My angels and to My saints :
" how right it is to love Him! "
then I shall draw you back again

45

into My nuptial chamber to show you
how I look after My own and make you
taste My sweet Love ..... why this shade
on your eyes, My love?

What will my own Orthodox people
say to all of this*!! Here You are,
pouring oil on me, behind and in front
of the walls of Your Sacred Heart,
yielding Your perfume on me, while
embracing me with Your right Arm.
They are not used to such talk!

they will get used to it as soon as
their soul goes to heaven .... do you want
that My Messages spread out quickly?

* Here I held my head in my two hands.

46

Yes Lord, I would like that no one
is prevented from hearing Your
Message; I want what You want:
I want that everyone lends an
ear to Your melodies, so that everyone can say: " I am like a son
and daughter to the Most High,
whose love for me surpasses
my mother's." (Si 4:10)

so come and be like a sensible daughter
and have your rest and replenish your
soul from the Sources of My Sacred Heart,
did you not hear before, how I take
care of My own? I want to train you
spiritually in My Body, and to
make you strong to love sincerely and

47

learn self-control; I am like a mother
feeding and looking after her own children;
you need feeding right now, My dove, to
gain strength and grow in My Love ....
I made you responsible for delivering
My Love Hymn to all nations and
you still have a long way to go; but
before you go out again, My sister,
you must remain for a while with your
eldest Brother to train your mind in
His* ♡ — I invite you now, in the nup-

---

* I knew that Jesus wanted now that I rest in a <u>retreat</u>
  in His Body, to recover my strength, physically and
  spiritually.

48

tial chamber of My Heart, even if you
are troubled or worried, My beloved, in
My Heart you will find your peace because
I will remind you that nothing ever
can come between you and My Love ♡
I will reveal My beauty to you so
that your soul succumbs to My charms,
then in your ardour to possess Me you
would offer yourself to Me, but then I,
I would have already sealed your forehead with My matrimonial kiss; show
Me your hands .... then look at Mine ....

49

come and have your pilgrimage in My Hands; My Hands have done many good works that are not recorded in The Book*; no king has ever been known to have served his subordinates as I, who am the King of kings, served; My state was divine, yet I did not cling to My equality with God but emptied Myself to assume the condition of a slave; (Phil: 2: 6-7) I shall know My own in this way,

---

* Jesus meant the Bible. As His Beloved disciple said: " There were many other things that Jesus did; if all were written down, the world itself I suppose, would not hold all the books that would have to be written. (Jn 21: 25)

50

when they will empty themselves and
follow My divine Will; give Me your hands,
My Vassula, so that I inscribe in them
My Instructions and the Work for your
salvation; I have anointed them
so that they in their turn, anoint the
sick and the weary; I have blessed
them that they offer Me good deeds unsparingly and I have kissed them
over and over again to give them
strength and continue to snatch souls
from the Evil one and bring them to

51

Me; My own Hands have shaped and modelled yours so that they offer Me incense and sacrifice; you will learn in this pilgrimage of My Hands how I served faithfully and performed works that no one has ever done; My beloved then will rest by My Springs* again; there, while your head will be leaning on My Royal Heart, your right

---

* Jesus means that after having gone out on a mission again, in the return of the journey, I would again lean on His Heart to rest, to restore my strength.

52

hand held in Mine, I will be crowning
you with My Love and Tenderness, filling your soul with consolations;
renewing you like an eagle, I will be refreshing you so that your years do not
dwindle away like a shadow; and
while My gaze would never be leaving
you, delighting to love she who loves
Me, remembering all those instants
when you were ever at play in My
Presence; and others when moved by
the Spirit you would cry out to Us:

53

" Abba!" I would be making sure that you would be continuing to be giving Me undivided attention and love; in My desire to be loved I will hold you captive in My Heart; and as a watchman posted on a tower I will look out for any intruders. I will be guarding you, My love, like the pupil of My Eye...! and you, in your delight noticing My eagerness to keep you for Myself, you would run to hide yourself in the shadow of My wings, like chicks running

54

to hide under the wings of their mother,
you would crouch in My warmth and
I would keep you in the warmth of My
Heart ♡ then, once again, I and you
would go out again, I will take you
in the garden of My Mouth, there
you will have your pilgrimage and
you will learn in this pilgrimage,
how distraught I could be when your
mouths who receive Me*, infect your
spirit and your soul by poisonous words

* Jesus means in the Eucharist.

55

on one another; learn from My Mouth
the Truth and proclaim only the Truth
all around, so let your mouth honour
Me, praising Me night and day; let
your mouth sing to Me, smile at Me,
let it sound like a million melodies
in My Ears, like the sweetest psalm of
the psalmist; let your mouth be like a
double edged sword, to pull down the
heresies and the traitors in My Church,
but among all those who thirst for
Me let your mouth be My echo and like

56

sweet wine, teaching everyone how to win My friendship; from My Mouth you will learn, My dove, Instructions, to speak as I wish you to speak and express thoughts according to My mind, then you will pass on these learnings to others without reserve; then again like a dove which would creep in its cote to have its rest, I would call you to rest in the nuptial chamber of My Heart, while My searching gaze would be in search of your eyes;

57

" My Lord, You look after me as nobody
     else does; you are my Inestimable
Treasure, and nobody and nothing else
in the whole world gives me so much
joy as You.
        One glance from You and my spirit
burns like fire, and my heart melts
like wax. One glance from You and
my soul is ravished by the depth
of Your Love; Your glance, my Holy
One is like a royal wedding song, it's
like the scent of a bouquet of lilies
wafted to me by the breeze, your
glance is like a Citadel with ivory
        towers all around....

daughter - of - the-King*, see how
your King is waiting to take His joy
in you? your God has anointed!

* Christ called me in an analogous name to mine, because Vassiliki means, ' daughter of the King ' too.

58

you with His Lips; My Lips are moist
with grace and My Lips will sing
songs of salvation to you so that we
repeat them together to the royal sons
and the royal daughters*¹ of the King,
that they may learn to give Us the right*²
praise and honour too; then .... the
days of virtues*³ will flourish filling the

*¹ God's whole creation; He indicates here that we are
of royal descent, of royal seed, since our Creator is King.

*² The Holy Trinity.

*³ The new heavens and the new earth, when God's
whole creation will be renewed in the coming
2nd Pentecost.

59

heavens and the earth with Our Glory *♡

My sister! let your eldest Brother now

carry you to have your pilgrimage in

His Eyes so that your soul may contem-

plate the perfect light, the principle

lamp of the body; I had said that

the lamp of your body is the eye and

that if your eye is sound, your whole

body will be filled with light, but that

if your eye is diseased, your whole body

will be all darkness; beware then

that the light inside you is not darkness

* Jesus said these words majestically filling me with hope.

60

lest you will be learned in evil and
you would not know it; the storm
wind itself is invisible, and when evil
works, it works in darkness to go un-
detected .... My Eyes have seen many
such things; for these pray and say:

" O Lord of all holiness,

     preserve for ever from all profanation

       Your sanctuaries* by purifying

     in Your Sacrificial Blood, their

---

* *1 Co 3:17 " The sanctuary of God is sacred; and you are that sanctuary."*

61

inner self from dead actions ♡ ; amen ; " — do not allow your eyes rest on any misconduct but lift them to heaven and I will show you the light of My triune Holiness to contemplate, each minute of your life, Our Face, that will be turned towards you ♡ enter into My Eyes*, so that you see things the way I see them, do not think that I will hide away from you those fearful sights that I bring Tears of Blood in

* Jesus is speaking in metaphors.

62

My Eyes; since I have brought you to live a true life in Me, I will show you these abominations so that you pray more; in My Body lives the fullness of divinity, and yet many of My Own are persecuting Me because of My divinity; use My Own Eyes* to read My Word to establish in you the perfection that comes through faith in Me; speak now to My Heart, My chosen one ....

* Jesus is speaking symbolically

63

What can I say? Of what can I speak to Your Heart? It is You who valued me beyond price; it is You who cured my eyes;*¹ My perfect One, it was You who told me of Your faithfulness; it was You Yourself who brought me to Your Royal Courts, to walk freely in them;

how I wanted to rank you with My own and give you My Body*² .... I wanted so much to heal your disloyalty and count you as one of My brides .... My burning desire was to make Myself known to you in a most intimate way and show

* symbolically * Jesus means the Holy Eucharist;

64

you the True God, the living God,
the everlasting King; ‘let* not this world
reduce My lily to silence, let not their
conspiracies affect her or touch her soul
but let My psalms continue to be for
her and for all those who hear them
like a wedding song, that they get to
know the Triune True God who is
Father of All; now My lily, I will

* Jesus with a firm but low voice, sounding
  like a command,   uttered the
  words that followed; He was like He
  was talking to Himself; like one says: "thinking
            aloud."

Excerpts from Notebook 89

28 January 97 (continued from Notebook #88)... "My Lord is great!" you may come now in the nuptial chamber of My Heart; (Note: every time our Good Lord invites me in the nuptial chamber, it is His invitation of a retreat...to be often alone with Him); p. 1.

✠ I imprinted My Holy Face on yours, Face on face, sealed for all eternity; pause and reflect on these words; p. 3.

✠ My ears are sensitive;...do not be reckless or deaf to the callings of the needy,...do not frown at them but offer them your hand; p. 7.

NB
89

18 February 97...To one so weak, what will I not give...not do...may your race with Me...be blessed, for it will save many souls; p. 15.

✠ Remind them that I will defend the poorest (poor in spirit); p. 15.

✠ I love you, child...look at Me then tell Me that you love Me too...try to imitate Me; fill yourself with My Love; p. 17.

3 April 97...Vassula's prayer: Release my feet from their nets and snares; turn to me; see how the wolves multiply? p. 18.

✠ Do not worry about them, I am with you...elevate, My child...your spirit in Mine...have you not noticed my victories? p. 18.

✠ With My cross in one hand and in the other My Word...I, your King, will be walking majestically by your side; p. 19.

✠ I will lean down from the heights of My Glory, to the dying (spiritually) yet so loved by me...to tell them how precious they are; p. 20.

4 April 97...Today, many of My own are raising...their sword against Me...the great fire now is ready to devour them; p. 23.

✠ There is a Mediator...He prays in man's place...to be spared; p. 24.

✠ Since this Work of Wisdom is lifted high...and exposes their iniquity, it has become their prime target; p. 26.

✠ Long for me...pursue Me...desire Me...delight in nothing...except our Triune Presence; p. 27.

✠ I observe My faithful servant (the Pope) while his lips mutter endless blessings for his persecutors; p. 29.

✠ Many of you...are waiting for exteriour signs...Jesus has warned you, not to...seek what is real and divine from within you; p. 36.

✠ My children, in your conversion you will discover the real glory of God who dwells and shines within you; p. 41.

✠ Today He is performing signs and marvels...God leans...from heaven to you; p. 43.

✠ I shall show My great Love to Wretchedness, and heal their wounds; p. 46.

✠ And you, daughter, carry out what God ordered you to do; p. 52.

12 April 97...Christ is risen...this is what God wants you to say...declare... that My Son is indeed resurrected; *p. 53.*

✠ Satan and his dark dominion are...bringing afflictions into families...raising false prophets...so the elect...fall; p. 55.

✠ False prophets are being poured on you like rain, bringing so much mischief and so much confusion; p. 56

24 April 97 (Jerusalem Prayer Group)...My beloved souls, you are My Gift; your presence here is a gift to Me;...may you be blessed; p. 58.

✠ My sister I am with you, My friends, remain with Me; p. 58.

6 May 97...Have you not noticed how I surrounded you with songs of deliverance? *p. 60.*

✠ I will sing this song which will be sung for all eternity and for all of you; p. 61.

✠ My fragile one, wander no more like a vagabond but allow Me to draw you in Me; ...you to whom I allied Myself by marriage; p. 61.

✠ I tell you...I will pay homage to you My bride...for having gone, for My sake, through hardships and persecutions...let this oil...heal all your imperfections...may your presence be so radiant and beautiful that it would draw many; p. 64.

give constant cause for you to say:
" My Lord is great!" you may come
now in the nuptial chamber of My Heart;*
have you not read:" joy for all
who take shelter in Me, endless shouts
of joy!" (Ps 5:11) and " my joy lies
in being close to God;" (Ps 73:28)
come to Me then, the Spouse invites
you, you who look after My Own Vine-
yard, come and prosper in My Presence,

---

* Every time our Good Lord invites me in the nuptial chamber, it is His invitation of a retreat, because He made me understand that He wants me to be
often alone with Him and only for Him.

2

and you will praise My Love above all; and again at the sight of the splendour of My Sacred Heart, your heart will succumb in My charms, remembering like an echo My appearance* in your childhood, when I exerted all My charms to draw you to Me, and while I was drawing you to Me, My citadel, I said: " I will refresh My citadel from the river of My

* The vision I had when I was a child. Jesus was smiling at me, I saw Him all the way to His waist. Every time He said: " come to Me;" I was drawn to Him by an invisible force. Then I was so close to Him that our faces met and I felt as though my face was absorbed by His Face.

3

Heart and I will sanctify this citadel to keep My dwelling place from falling;" and your King exhaled on you His Breath like a delicate fragrance, then without any further delay I imprinted My Holy Face on yours, Face on face, sealed for all eternity; pause a while and reflect on these words.... may My words give you pleasure....

You are my Master now and so I bow to You; teach me what is pleasing to You so that all I will do may be acceptable to You; my reasonings are unsure

4

and this citadel, which You call,
is out of clay and it weighs down
the teaming mind; You say, My
King, that You have imprinted Your
Image on mine;

yes*; and while doing so, I then planted a kiss
on those lips which would become My Echo
and would proclaim the Truth, to train
them to hymn My Name and say:
" sing to the Prince-of-Peace,
sing to the Immortal One, to
the Mighty God; open your hearts

* Like I said before, in the vision of Christ, I was
drawn near Him, until my face was stuck on
His and it was as though my face went through
His Face.

5

and let them be consumed by
His jealous Love; sing to the
Lord and King, and exult at His
coming;" come, let your eyes now,
My beloved, feast on the fathomless treasures
of My Heart; then the All Powerful One
will carry you to have your pilgrimage
in My Ears .... you will learn how to
listen and understand shrewd proverbs,
My love; if you lend an ear, you will
learn from Wisdom, and will thirst
for any discourse coming from Me,

6

you will learn in the garden of My Ears
how My Ears are opened to anyone who
invokes Me sincerely, and comes to Me *
in purity of heart repenting like a loud
lamentation book; insisting on their wretchedness, their unworthiness, and on how
they had failed Me; at this sound, My
Heart leaps from its place; that sound
of contrition will lead them to My Courts;
so that your ears listen to My Voice,

* I understood here that Jesus was including confes-
sors and not only Himself.

7

you would have to lower your voice;
come and learn how I respond and free
the wretched and the poor who call Me;
appeal to Me and My Ears will hear
your appeal and I will come and
save you, I will hear your calling;
My Ears are sensitive; and you, as
a creature, do not be reckless or deaf
to the callings of the needy, but open
your ears to their appeal; do not
frown at them but offer them your
hand; do you not know how I shudder

8

when an appeal is made and My creatures do not give a hearing or answer to the supplicant; My Sacred Heart aches in My Breast; in the gardens of My Ears, you will learn how, your God, is looking down from His Throne at the sons and daughters of men, leaning towards them with His Ear stuck on their lips; and you, who have seen thousands of myriads of angels surrounding My Glorious Throne*, tell them:

* I understood also His Sacred Heart.

9

" come and listen : I was instructed
by the Holy One to tell you what
He has done for me : when I
uttered my cry of metanoia* to Him
and high praise was on my tongue,
had I been guilty after my metanoia
in my heart still, the Lord would
never have heard me; but God not
only heard me, He listened to my
appeal and responded to my
prayer; blessed be God, triune

* repentance

10

in His Holiness, who neither ignored my prayer nor deprived me of His Love;" this is what you are going to tell them * now come and step into your permanent Home, the nuptial chamber of My Heart where your King is waiting to rejoice in you and you in Him; come My angel and My bride, I am longing to dress you with My Name, with My very Presence; your

* The Holy One asked me to look at Psalms 66, verses 16-20.

11

clothing will be Me for I am everything; in My Body lives the fullness of Divinity, therefore in Me, you will find your fulfilment ♡ I will have you hidden in Me, and in this manner, when the Time comes, I will present you to the Father ♡ I am your sweet fragrance, Vasula, and I want you to be like a bright star shining in the darkness of this generation, perfuming it * with My fragrance; you will continue to shine because you

* the generation

12

would be offering the world what came from My Mouth *, you would be offering everyone : the word of Life ; and many would see Me in you *; since I have clothed you with My Name, so that you become truly My companion ; your True God, your Lord Jesus Christ welcomes you wholeheartedly now in His Sacred Heart : your Home .... I have revealed My Dominion to you, My sister,

* Christ's Holy Face appearing in the place of my face.

13

My own .... My grace is with you ic
*¹ and My favour binds you to Us ....
*² and in Me, We have favoured you
to see what man is unable to see on
his own ♡ We give you Our Peace ...

A Ⓧ Ω

The above message was given to me with
many intervals in between. It has taken
50 pages.

*¹ Suddenly God the Eternal Father spoke
*² The Holy Spirit then spoke

14

18. 2. 97

My Psalm & my Hymn,
My Amen,
My Brother, my Sister and Friend
My Father and Mother,
My Sweet Fragrance and my Incense,
My Sunshine and my Light,
My Brilliant Flame never ceasing
to shine,
My series of Banquets,
My Safety and Rock
of my Strength,
My Increase and my Wealth,
My Portal of Eternity,

What makes You leap with joy at
the sight of this speck of dust
passing by You?

its absolute nothingness makes My
Heart leap with such delight

15

that I draw the attention of My Angels
who surround Me;

you and you only are
my Cup ...

to one so weak, what will I not give ....
what will I not do .... may your race
with Me in the world be blessed, for
it will save many souls; let even the
mountains and hills bow low in hearing My Canticle of peace given to My
people; remind them that I will
defend the poorest*; tell them that

* poor in spirit.

16

'in your days virtue will begin to flourish, and a universal peace will soon cover My creation for My empire shall stretch from sea to sea; and the Beast will cower before My Presence and your enemies who are My enemies will grovel in the dust, the Amen is on His way to purify with devouring flame every race because I hate the practices of the apostate; the heavens are at work now, so wear Me like a rich vestment to announce, in our journey, the Amen's

17

words; follow Me in My footprints which are soaked with My Blood; I love you, child, turn around and look at Me then tell Me that you love Me too

♡ love does not come to an end with Me, My Love is everlasting and secure; try then to imitate Me; fill yourself with My Love; I, Jesus, bless you

ΙΧΘΥΣ 🐟

3. 4. 97

Lord of Peace,
watch over my soul
and be my protection

18

from the wolves that hound me
for proclaiming all Your wonders
    and for announcing my
love for Your House;
    Release my feet from their nets
and snares;   turn to me;   see
how the wolves multiply?
    See their violence?   With loud
cries they denounce me, tearing me
    to pieces in front of Your Eyes;
They think out false accusations,
    their mouths wide to accuse me;

do not worry about them, I am with

you; My Peace and Love I give you;

elevate, My child, child of My Heart,

your spirit in Mine and do not fall;

have you not noticed My victories? *

* Assemblies being fuller than ever, in my prayer meetings

19

My glory shines within and without these Messages; remain devout to Me, prayerful, and effaced so that I am seen wherever you go;* in this way we could advance, you, with My cross in one hand and in the other one, My Word, which will be your lamp, while I, your King, will be walking majestically by your side and victorious, gloriously accumulating My trium—phs in your faithfulness, while My

* This is symbolic but also literally too, when Christ appears in my face, effacing me entirely.

20

glorious sceptre in My Hand will keep directing your steps where they should tread and where I wish you to go in My Name; we will descend even more now to encounter those who are in the vile depths of sin, to teach them forgiveness, kindness, mercy, love, faith, hope, and I will lean down from the heights of My Glory, to the dying*, yet so loved by Me .... to cure them, to console them and tell them how

* spiritually

21

precious they are to Me; all will vanish
one day and wear out like a garment,
but My Love for them will be unchan-
geable .... lean now, My dearest, on My
Sacred Heart so that every heart-beat
you hear anoints your soul like fresh
oil, renewing you and refreshing you;
and while you will be leaning on My
Royal Heart, you will be drinking from
Its flowing stream, a living water which
will turn into a spring inside you,
welling up to eternal life; be stead-

22

fast in heart, for I am your Salvation!
I bless you in My Triune Holiness, three
times;

4 . 4 . 97

flower - of - My - Heart listen to My words;
I am asking you: do you believe in
what is written in Scriptures?

Why Lord, of course I do!

do you believe that God can speak to
man?

You prospered me by speaking to
me, so how could I not believe You
spoke to me?

23

today many of My own are raising in
My very House their sword against Me ....
being swollen with pride they say:
" we are gods ; " they claim to be so
much greater than all that men call
' god ', so much greater than anything
that is worshipped, that they enthrone
themselves in My Sanctuary and claim
that they are God ; every word
proclaimed by Me is rejected by those
very ones, but the great fire now is
ready to devour them .... they claim that

24

they have grasped the mystery of Myself,
there is a Mediator* to remind man
where his duty lies, to take pity on him,
He prays in man's place to be restored,
and spared from the pit; all this I
do again and yet again for man, res-
cuing his soul from the eternal fires
and letting the light of life shine bright
on him .... to conceal their plans these
people, who raise Me daily, scheme in the
dark to overthrow Peter's Chair and

* I think Jesus was speaking of His Holy Spirit.

25

silence the Vicar of My Church and all
those to whom I revealed their plans and
expose their apostasy; they scheme in the
dark to silence Me, saying : ' who can see
us? who can recognize us?' but the
lowly rejoice when they hear and recognize
My Voice ; the poorest exult in My Presence;
— their* sacrifices to Me are a mockery now;
why, they have become the very Thing of
Shame in My Courts; these wrong-
doers in My House are speculating to
shut My Voice ; they will try and im-

* God talks about the apostates now.

26

pose an order on all of you, to condemn
the magnificant works of Wisdom,
since this*¹ Work of Wisdom is lifted
high like a luminary banner and exposes
their iniquity, it has become their
prime target; My*² fairest heritage has
become like a woman betraying her
lover .... and to you, whom I opened
your ear to hear Me and become My
pupil, I tell you: do not fear,

＊ Meaning the messages of True Life in God.
＊ Here, Jesus was like speaking to Himself.

27

long for Me as never before so that it
becomes your sweet intoxication, since it
will be sweeter than wine;
pursue Me, so that in the end you will
find the Knowledge of God and His Wisdom,
wholeheartedly desire Me, just like an
orphan desires his parents, desire Me with
all your heart; delight in nothing else
on earth nor in heaven except in
Our Triune Presence, let your joy lie in
being close to Us who have espoused you
to Our Holiness for Our Glory but

28

also for your sanctification ♡

My God, my God, now is the time
to act, for Your Law is being
broken and evil is gaining power
in your House; I am finding that
the Abomination is spreading, just
like rivers swamping their foundations, it is swamping us; Triune
God and Guarantor of our well-
being, come to our rescue!

I will fulfill My Promise and your distress
and anguish will come to an end; so tell
My sons and daughters that My Voice will
soon thunder from above and the foundations of the mountains will tremble;

29

now these traders in My Church are
closing in on him whom I placed on
Peter's Chair and have eyes for nothing
but to see him overthrown; they look
like a lion eager to tear to pieces, like
a young lion crouching in its hide; I
observe these very ones who want to silence
My Voice,*¹ each of their moves, and the
sight of their moves disgust Me; I
observe My faithful servant *² while his

*¹ Those who want to ban forever locutions
   to call them simple meditations.
*² Meaning the Pope.

30

lips mutter endless blessings for his persecutors ; I listen to his voice while he
is being struck on his back :*" in Your
Love, my Redeemer, listen to my plea;
my cruel persecutors are closing in, how
remote they are from Your Law!
here I am, up before dawn to call for
Your help : salve Regina, come to our
help, miserere ...... come to our help,
O God! Guardian of souls come to our

* This shows the manner of the Holy Father's fervent
contempletive prayer; the words are not necessarily the
Pope's words verbatim.

31

help ; Madre de Dios, Bride of the Holy Spirit, may my cry reach Your presence and touch Your maternal Heart; O pure One, seated by the Father, the Son and the Holy Spirit, Celestial Throne of God, take up my cause and bring us universal peace .... pity us .... pity Your children ....
I open my mouth panting with hope as You unfold Your mantle spreading it on the suffering, on the wretched, on the poor and the forlorn, to protect us You give us streams of Light and Hope,

32

and my distress diminishes ; as a small child near his mother, I am reassured, as a small child near his mother, I take my refuge and put my hope in You, Celestial Throne of the most Holy Trinity ♡ Mediatrix of all graces, save us from the tempestous floods of sin, multiply Your graces and turn the hearts of parents towards their children and the hearts of children towards their parents; O Mother of Divine Love, I ask Your Royal Heart, ever filled with graciousness and goodness to

33

remember me to the Father; I will count
no credit for myself since it was You,
my Guarantor, who, in Your loving
tenderness saved my life that day,*
so that I would shepherd the sheep entrusted to me; Virtuous Virginal Heart of
Mary, pity Your children and open the
Gate of Your Heart on the exiled, shed-
ding Your Light on us all; Mother
of the disciples, Mother of Triumph, Mother
of unequalled Redemption, Mother of the

* The attempt to kill the Pope.

34

prophets and charisms, Mother of the
  True Vine, may my entreaties reach
Your Maternal Heart'; in Your Love,
listen to my cry .... my God, Guar-
dian of souls', I put my hope in You....
O God, how I love Your Law!" amen;

  So now break Your silence, Lord,
turn Your ear to his prayers and hear
what he says. Send us from on high
this Living Water to cleanse us
            purifying us.

dawn <u>will</u> come after this endless night
Vassula, My friend, and the Glory of
Our Triune Holiness will shine;

35

(Our Holy Mother speaks). and I, your Holy Mother, salute you, Vassula, yes, Our Hearts* will rise like the dawn to brighten the earth in its present gloom; Our Hearts in their triumph will shine on mankind brighter in radiance than all the constellations put together, more resplendent than a thousand suns, and the people who had been walking now for years, in darkness, will see from the heavens a great light; on those who

* Jesus and Mary's Heart

36

lived in a land of shadow, a light
will shine; many of you, little children,
are waiting for exteriour signs and exteriour prodigies and portents; many of
you turn your gaze upwards searching
the skies, and yet, My Son, Jesus,
has warned you, not to seek exteriour
signs but to seek what is real and
    divine from within you ♡ many of
you read and re-read this prophetic
revelation with eyes but never see,
because when you read, you read with

37

the sole interest of finding extraordinary
signs or indications on prodigies and
portents, instead of calling the Holy Spirit
to endow upon you a spirit of discernment and perception to penetrate rather
into the mystery of Christ and into
the mystery of His Resurrection and
enable your soul to progress spiritually
to reach the promised land .... if anyone continues to set his mind and heart
in that manner, My poor children, the
day when you will be face to face

38

with your Creator, you will be standing
in front of His Throne empty-handed
because your soul will be still a
wilderness, a parched land, a desert;
but if you penetrate with the right
heart into the Mysteries We reveal to
you now in these Messages, you will
start to understand that every
work that God is doing is full of
glory and majesty: when He adorns,
with His Majesty, a soul and
turns that soul to enter into His

39

Kingdom and into Heaven, you will, then, commemorate <u>this</u> marvel because you would see its Glory; when God provides the starved and those who fear Him with Celestial Food, so that they too could inherit and become heirs of His Kingdom and are framed in faithfulness and integrity, you will commemorate <u>this</u> prodigy too, because you will recognize His Blessing and you will wear around your neck this Blessing like one wears a garland;

40

when His Works of Wisdom which
are like an Infinite sea, shining like a
thousand suns will illumine your soul
radiantly, so that the fruit on your
lips increases and that every word
pronounced by your lips will be
like a consuming fire, purifying this
earth, on that day and night you
will never stop singing hymns to the
Amen for His abundant goodness,
patience and tolerance He had for
you all these years of your wilderness,

41

your soul will commemorate these prodigies, portents and signs every day of your life; that is why, My children, in your conversion you will discover the real glory of God who dwells and shines within you; unveil your eyes to see that your Creator lives also within you, who embraces you in His Love; your Maker is also your Spouse*¹ too for He is the Head*² of every creature ... pray,

*¹ Is 54:5   *² Rm 7:4 + 1 Co 11:3

42

My children, for those whose hearts are away from God; many of them say: "let us eat and drink today, to-morrow we shall be dead,* come, let us feast now while we are alive, our life will pass away like wisps of cloud, yes, our days here are number-ed and will pass by like a shadow, so let us feast!" and they go on disgracing themselves and the Image of God, sinking deeper and deeper

* *Is* 22:13

43

into sin, unaware that they are more
dead than alive .... ah, so many of
them have been misled by their own
presumption, and wrong-headed opinions
have warped their ideas .... My Son,
Jesus Christ, Redeemer of mankind, has
the power to save everyone, for the
Father, your Creator, has given Him the
power over all mankind; today He is
performing signs and marvels as no
other time in history; God leans all
the way from heaven to you, My

TRUE LIFE IN GOD

44

children; your King, Jesus, has placed His Crown aside and descended from His Glorious throne to reach you; this King, who was seated on His Royal throne, dressed in fearful splendour, glittering with His Glory more than gold and precious stones; raised His Face, full of graciousness and afire with majesty looked on the throng of angels surrounding Him; He looked on His Saints, and on the whole Heavenly Court and said, His Heart

45

afire with love: " I have resolved to open My reserves*¹ of Heaven and pour out on this reckless generation My hidden Manna*², a treasure reserved for these times, when the world would turn cold and away from the love of God - in

*¹ At the same time I heard the word' resources.'
*² While these words were pronounced : ' hidden manna', I understood too : " the hidden treasures of the Sacred Heart on which St Gertrude the Great was permitted to have a glimpse, and was told that these treasures are kept for those times when people would grow cold in the love of God. That is, when Jesus will reveal His Treasure. These times are now.

46

its coldness of heart;*[1] let it be known now that the godless will be fed from these reserves; why, I, Myself, will go to them with comforting words and soothe the wretched; I shall show My great love to Wretchedness, and heal their wounds;*[2] I, Myself, will speak to them and tell them that I am their brother and their Divine friend who could bring back their divinity; in

*[1] What I had understood, it was confirmed.
*[2] Wounds on our soul from sin.

47

the bitterness of their slavery, they, one after the other will ask themselves:

" how have I come to be counted as one of the children of the Most High, I, who am the vermin of the vermins, a vermin among vermins? how can this most Glorious God look at me twice and assign a place for me among His Saints? how can this glorious Sun rise and shine on us too?" " no vermin, no; you will not die; your King will not let you die, I will save you by

48

My Hand, little vermin, and I will come to your help so that you too may be able to appear in My Courts one day ♡ I will change your loathsomeness into a festival, for your King is near you now*, and from a festival I will transform you into a paradise, a glorious heaven so that I, in

---

* this reminded me of the first words my angel Daniel pronounced regarding God. In 1985 he said: "God is near you, and loves you." — This meant that it would be the beginning of my conversion that would come through His grace.

49

My Magnificence can be praised and glorified; and in this heaven you will invoke Me and seek My Ways from there on so that you may live; My Omnipotent Breath will breathe on you My fragrance; no one knows all the marvels that are inside heaven, and how I can make My Will be known on earth as it is in heaven ♡ to lift you, vermin, whether important or ordinary, rich or poor, I will open My Lips and from My Mouth I will pour out on you, vermin, My

50

delicate ointment * anointing each one of you "; yes, I will come and free them, to take heart, I will show them My wonderful works, reminding them of their inheritance, offering them My Kingdom .... in My Infinite Clemency I will bow down from heaven and with My gold sceptre lift those scarcely born to follow Me

---

* Sg. 1:3 " Your Name is like an oil poured out, and that is why the maidens love You. "

Jesus means: by pouring out His ointment on the sinners, they will be healed; in other words, ointment represents His Name and once His Name comes on the sinners it brings them to love God.

51

in My traces; many will look uncompre-
hending on My choice and that grace
and mercy can be given too to those who
once had ceased to be; — I will descend all the way to them and go as
far as to the remotest lands, and mix
Myself among them; and they will praise
My love above wine saying to Me:
    "how right it is to love You,
Sovereign of the Universe!" * then
full of graciousness He lifted His right

* Then our Lady continued.

52

Hand and blessed the earth; and you, daughter, carry out what God ordered you to do, see how much brighter your eyes are now that you have eaten this mouthful of 'honey*¹? fill your mouth with oil*² and go with My blessings, I am with you ♡

---

*¹ Our Lady meant: Celestial Manna which represents here, the Word of God.
*² Oil represents, the Name of God, here.
"Your Name is an oil poured out," Sg 1:3

53

12. 4. 97

My peace I give you, Vassula, come and hear your Holy Mother: the Word of the Almighty has indeed been addressed to you; come now, you whom God's message was entrusted; come and write this:

"Christos Annesti!" *Alithos Annesti!* *

yes, Christ is risen, and this is what God wants you to say to everyone; declare to this dying world that My Son has

* In Greek: Christ has risen. The response: 'Truly He has risen'. Greeting used usually for 40 days after the celebration of the Resurrection Day in Easter.

54

indeed resurrected; preach a resurrected
Christ, My angel, because many in
your generation do not acknowledge this
truth because of their rationalism;
have you not read: ' these same people
boast of their worldly achievements,
thinking they have everything they want
and that they are in glory 'while' possessing the worldly kingdoms'; they are
filled with their own importance instead of the fullness of the triune
God; this is why the earth is in

True Life in God

55

a turmoil and so much innocent blood
is shed; but these are also the signs
of the times; Satan and his dark dominion are spitting out on the earth
their vomit bringing afflictions into
families and divisions too; they are raising false prophets around the world
producing signs and portents as well,
but this is so that the elect too may
fall in their treachery; those false
prophets are being poured on you like
rain, bringing so much mischief and

56

so much confusion, My poor children ....
words and false oaths fill their mouths
and their prophecies are like
poisonous weeds that thrive now in
the furrows of the Lord's field; their
roots are spreading to bring forth new
poisonous weeds; the danger signals echo
in your ears, My children, but you
do not seem to understand
or discern those signals; they
search for the wind that will
carry their voices higher than

57

King Solomon's, the prophet Elijah's or 'Moses', declaring themselves stupendously greater*, by crowning themselves and asking themselves : " is it not wonderful to have so much power ? " be warned, lest you be deceived and may God endow your hearts with discernment, so that His Glory given before your eyes, draws you into the Truth ♡

* Our Blessed Mother is giving us a warning for those that declare themselves greater than Solomon, or those who go around saying that they are Elija or Moses, or Enoch. Then there are the other souls in total illusion dragging many to read their illusions, and follow them.

58

Jerusalem — 24. 4. 97

(While praying in the prayer group of True Life in God, in Jerusalem, Christ called me to receive the following message.)

My beloved souls, you are My gift; your presence here is a gift to Me; your prayers are a caress on Me, may you be blessed .... and you,* your tears are a soothing balm on My Wounds, My sister ♡ I am with you, My friends, remain with Me; ic

* Jesus was speaking to a nun who was present.

59

6. 5. 97

My Lord, my Cup,
            my Banquet,
I lack nothing in Your Presence,
Blessed be Your Name thrice holy;

Down in the dust I laid,
        until Your Word came to my ear
and revived me; then, in Your great
        Love and Compassion, You kissed
my eyes to open them;   I began to see;
        I saw beyond the zenith of the
stars and beheld in my heart Your
Magnificence;

I saw the Invisible God, and the
One who was Inaccessible to my touch
was suddenly all around me and within me!
        the Impenetrable instantly became
penetrable with a simple utterance
        from His Mouth, the Intercessor
within me lifted my spirit in a cloud
and together with Him and through
Him, brought my soul in

60

full communion with You, to
penetrate into the very depths
of Your Majesty.

My Vassula, I laid down My Love before
your very eyes * ♡ have you not noticed
how I surrounded you with songs of
deliverance? — would you like Me to
sing to you one more of My songs?

O yes! I would like You to sing to
me and for me an endless song.

* When Jesus was explaining Himself to me
He used a gesture with His Hands. He had
both His Hands lifted as if carrying someone
then lowered them all the way down
as if He put gently down someone.

61

I will sing this song* which will be sung for all eternity and for all of you; and you, My beloved, you may be My harp and My lyre, accompanying My Voice; come, come and tell your soul: "Jesus is my salvation"; (Title of Jesus' song.) I am your salvation; see how I come with My delicate fragrance of incense and myrrh all the way to your room? My fragile one, wander no

* The message of Love from Jesus are songs. God's Word is so beautiful that it becomes a canticle to the soul.

62

more like a vagabond but allow Me to draw you in Me; enjoy My Presence, enjoy My great wealth of My Heart, you to whom I allied Myself by marriage; I have become your royal counsellor; now and then, to hearten you, I shall show Myself*[1]; do not ask: "who is this like a column of light*[2]?" before the dawn —

---

*[1] When Christ appears in my face, effacing my face entirely. Many people gave their testimonies on this phenomenon.

*[2] One night, when everything else in the room was dark, I saw near me 2 columns of a dazzling brightness. like a mirror sparkling in the sun, but not hurting the eyes. I feared; then I heard: " do not fear; " and it vanished.

63

wind rises, before the shadows flee, come closer to your Beloved and take your shelter in His embrace, then your soul will rejoice in His embrace; no one will disturb your rest; no one can touch your rest in My Heart because I will safely guard you, My beloved; no one will dare disturb you, no one will dare approach you when they will see from afar the flare in My Eyes of My jealous love, guarding you jealously; I shall let My jealous love speak out

TRUE LIFE IN GOD

64

now: as David said in his psalm:
"You anoint my head with oil,"
I tell you, with My Heart in My
Hand: I will pay homage to you
My bride by anointing your head again
with oil for having gone, for My
sake, through hardships and persecutions;
let this oil, My loved one, cover your
head and heal all your imperfections,
and as a lily among the thistles, may
your presence be so radiant and
beautiful that it would draw many

Excerpts from Notebook 90

6 May 97 (continued from Notebook 89)...I, for My part, will stir their love to long for Me; I will rouse their thirst; p. 1.

✠ I will take it as My prime and personal concern to preserve My Throne in your heart; p. 1.

✠ Let your spirit boast of the one true Knowledge...rejoice for having Me... as close to your heart as one can be; p. 3.

✠ I, Jesus, am your salvation and your Holy Companion, the One who is singing to you, is hidden with you and within you; p. 4.

✠ So lift your eyes...and look at the One who laid down His Life for you; p. 5.

✠ <u>This</u> is the wealth of My Sacred Heart...that will bring many nations back to Me...the wealth...will keep flowing to you; p. 5.

NB 90

✠ I have anointed you to go out and proclaim that I am renewing My creation...that My Return is imminent; p. 6.

✠ I will send you My Mother to be always by your side; p. 8.

✠ The Author and Composer of this song is He in whom you will live for all eternity, were you to follow Him; p. 10.

✠ I, the Lord, do not reject mankind... My favours are not all past; p. 12.

✠ My Father and I have made Our home with you, ("We espoused you to Us,") because of the greatness of the love you have for Me; p. 13.

✠ I am with you and will take delight while you perform your other works for your family; p. 13.

21 May 97 (Vassula asked "why this upheaval?")...Because your hand is unmasking all the enemies who infiltrated in My Church; p. 15.

✠ Do not worry about the wicked; the day will come when they will be expelled from My Courts;...you shall not draw the sword; p. 16.

✠ Trust Me...I will remain with you...till the end; you captivated your King by your wretchedness...you were captivated by ALL that I Am and that <u>you</u> are not; p. 17.

5 June 97 (True Life in God gathering in Greece)...Resound My Voice to the ends of the earth; let <u>everyone</u> hear and learn that I am a God of tenderness and mercy; p. 20

✠ Freedom is...in My Spirit thrice Holy;...My gift is... understanding...so that you will get to know Me as your Father; p. 21.

23 June 97 (Japan)...Father, in Your faithful love, turn towards Japan...let this nation become a hymn to the Hymn; p. 23.

✠ Speak My Vassula when I speak, be My Lips and glorify Me; p. 25.

13 August 87...My Heart could never fail you...you have become the child of Our Divine Love;...keep your mind locked in My Mind...prosper from within, My love; p. 26.

9 September 97...(Rhodos-Greece) I tell you: love the One who loves you most and who never fails you; p. 28

✠ So many of you are locked in the same sleep, a sleep of apathy! ask Me to forgive your past ill-will...I shall give you a pillar of light to illumine your dreadful night; p. 30.

25 September 97...Know My little Vassula, that the poor will receive more from Wisdom than the rich, who glory in their glory which is no glory at all; p. 41.

✠ From My Lips you will hear no flattery but righteousness; p. 43.

✠ <u>I, Yahweh, your Creator, am wedded to My creation and am everyone's Spouse</u>...how can I make this lot who cannot tell their right hand from their left hand, understand that...all I want from them is love, not sacrifice;...for how long are you going to chase the wind? p. 44.

✠ Have your retreat in My Heart...I am imprinting My words on you, for the salvation of so many sinners; p. 49.

✠ I have washed your hands...so that cleansed...they would write My Words and keep My books...write: I wish you to bear witness to My Holiness...be...a book written by the Triune God; p. 57.

I.

souls into the nuptial chamber of My
Heart, so that they too may rejoice
within Me, witnessing all My blessedness in
days to come; then with songs of exult-
ation they will bless My Holy Name;
and I, for My part, will stir their love
to long for Me; I will rouse their
thirst to seek My Heart alone ♡ as
a king who sits on his royal throne,
dressed in all his robes of state, glittering
with gold and precious stones, with a
sceptre in his right hand, I will take

2

it as My prime and personal concern to
preserve My Throne in your heart, so
that your heart will continue to be
adorned with the wealth of your King
and Lord; this wealth of knowing
Me in My triune glory; the wealth
of fearing Me and the wealth of shun-
ning every kind of sin, and final-
ly, the wealth of doing My Divine Will
and what is pleasing to Me, your God...
My travelling companion, repose now in
My embrace and allow yourself to be

3

carried in My Arms; allow yourself to be caressed and kissed; no one will dare disturb your repose when they will meet My Eyes; and if anyone*' were to be so rash as to challenge Me, My Breath will blow him away, grinding him to powder *²♡ come, let your spirit absorb the secrets of Wisdom, let your spirit boast of the one true Knowledge I, Myself, have given you; let your spirit rejoice for having Me, the

* / understood, evil intruders.
There was a tone of humour in His Voice when He said these words.

4

only Son, who am nearest to the Father's Heart as close to your heart as one can be; let your spirit absorb My Sweetness;

I, Jesus, am your salvation and your Holy Companion, the One who is singing to you, is hidden with you and within you; I am He; * My Vassula, consider the great number of gifts I have given you to appoint you not only as My bearer but also as My most precious bride; cultivated by My Word, disciplined by

* Jn 18: 6 + 8

5

My Wisdom, endowed by My Spirit and courted by My Royal Heart, rejoice! rejoice and be glad, that I, Jesus, am your Salvation! so lift your eyes, My loved one, lift your eyes and look at the One who laid down His Life for you; do not listen to those who talk nonsense and are filled with treachery; they have never met Me and they do not even know Me; but My glory has risen on you and through you into many hearts; this is the wealth of My Sacred Heart

6

long foretold, a wealth that will bring many nations back to Me and into My Courts; so lift your eyes and look at your glorious King; your ever tender Lover; with this sight of splendour, you will grow radiant, since the wealth of My Heart will keep flowing to you like a sea to enable you to continue My Work in graciousness; I have anointed you to go out and proclaim that I am renewing My creation, My loved one, and that My Return is imminent; but

7

for the moment, I and you, will go out again to the nations, especially where there is more wilderness than there is life; let Me renew your strength in My Heart by filling your heart with My Peace; we shall appear together again when the time comes; My victories, conquering souls will be hailed at every one of My steps, and you, fastened to Me, will run and not grow weary, will talk and not get thirsty, you will stand and never tire ♡ you will advance with

TRUE LIFE IN GOD

8

Me, your feet scarcely touching the ground while I will be lifting your hand to bless My people in My Name thrice Holy ♡ I am now holding you, My chosen one, by your right hand to clothe you with My richest clothes; I will clothe you with Myself; when you are dressed with Myself, these vestments will give you great fortitude in times of suffering; they will console you in times of hardships and distress, and to accompany them I will send you My

9

Mother to be always by your side;
in Her Graciousness, She will lead you
to reach perfection of holiness in the
fear of God ♡ now, delight Me and
bind My Words ever to your heart so
that whatever you will do, you will
do it with dignity and honour since
you have been assigned by the King
of Kings, and if anyone asks you:
"who is the composer of this song?"
answer them saying: it is Me who lives
in the heights of Glory; it is Me, the

10

very One who in His triune Holiness breathed into you life; it is He who said to the Samaritan woman;" the Water that I shall give will turn into a spring in him welling up to eternal life"; it is He who will say to the vast quantities of dry bones: " dry bones, hear the word of the Word, replenish yourselves with My Breath and rise!" say to them My sister and My beloved :" the Author and Composer of this song is He in whom you will live for all eternity, were you to follow Him "; breath of My Breath, flame of My Eyes, do not weary writing but keep your ear glued on My Breast; not even solemn festivals done in My honour, could come close enough and sur- pass those precious moments when I am with you and when you are opened to Me as a book so that I write in you My Love Hymn; this Love Hymn where He who is the Unknown to the unknown*, will be revealed to them in the fullness of His Glory; for I, the

* One is "unknown" to God when one does not do God's Divine Will, for they too have not met God. (Mt 7: 21-23)

12

Lord, do not reject mankind and My favours are not all past; this is what the unknown shall say with great joy:

" Jesus is my Salvation !"

God is your Friend, My Vassula, He who has knowledge of all things is your Friend; the One whom you invited at your table is your Faithful and Loyal Friend; let the nations know this, that they may learn who is the One that is standing now at their door, knocking; if they hear Me and open

13

their door to Me, I will come in and
share their meal side by side with them;
then, I, in My turn, when the time
comes, I will show My gratitude to
them, by inviting them to share My
Throne in heaven;

Lord, You are Great, You are
Glorious, wonderfully Strong, unconquer-
able. May Your whole creation
serve You in righteousness!

My Father and I have made Our home
with you*, because of the greatness

* I understood that this was like telling me:
"We espoused you to Us."

14

of the love you have for Me .... ah, Vassula, I still have many things to say to you but now it is time for you to complete your other duties too; I am with you and will take delight while you perform your other works for your family; since your birth, My loved one and during your childhood, My Eyes never ceased watching with delight, the one whom My Sacred Heart had chosen to make out of her, one day, a Tree; daughter—

15

of-the-Son,* I love you; eternal life
is to know Me, the only True God;

come ♡   A ⨉ Ω

21. 5. 97

Lord, Scriptures say: " the poor will
receive as much as they want to eat."
(Ps. 22: 26) Today You are filling our
starved mouths with Your Word, so
why this upheaval from Your House?

because your hand is unmasking all
the enemies who infiltrated in My

* The name Vassiliki means also: daughter-of
the-King. When Jesus used this term,
I understood, as He is King, that He
called me by my name in a symbolic way.

16

Church;

But they toss their head and sneer
at Your Words;

do not worry about the wicked; the
day will come when they will be expelled
from My Courts;* but you, you shall
not draw the sword ....

You offered me a vision the other day,
and You seemed so happy, so full
of Joy!

I was looking at My beloved ....

Ah! what can I say?

* I am not sure whether they are Courts of
heaven or if God meant here, the Church.

17

My Name.....

Jesus Christ, beloved Son of God
and Saviour.

be confident as much as you were confident that day; trust Me when
I said to you that no matter what
happens, I will remain with you in
this way till the end; let My Heart
take always this pleasure in you....*

in your innocence of course, do you
enjoy this journey with Me?

* I had not understood, then He added the rest.

18

My King ... can a King clothed
in His Majesty and Glory, wrapped in
a robe of light and splendour,
enjoy, as You appear to be enjoying, the company of a worm?

you captivated your King by your
wretchedness; and you, You were
captivated by All that I Am and
that you are not;

You came to someone of no repute,
You filled the starving with good things,
I mean to praise You all my life.

My beloved will perform My pleasure
with Me and I, I will hold you fast
near My Heart; have you not read:

19

" if a man is innocent, I will bring him freedom " ...*

* no, do not say anything just now, just love Me .... love for Love, heart for Heart ♡ let love lift your soul to Me ♡   ΙΧΘΥΣ ><>

Greece - Rhodos - 5. 6. 97

This message was given to the True Life in God Association members that gathered. There were 23 nationalities and 140 people.

My Lord, Your Word is
a Lamp for my feet,

* Jb 22:30   * I was about to say something.

20

Your Presence is the Joy and
Peace of my heart;

Saviour of mankind, what can
I do to be pleasing in Your
Eyes? What return could I make
to Yahweh, my Father,
for His generosity to me?

peace be with you*... resound My Voice
to the ends of this earth; let
everyone hear and learn that I am a
God of tenderness and mercy; My
people, My own, seek Me with all
your heart and avert your eyes from
the world, lift them up to Me and

* The Father speaks.

21

fix your gaze on your Creator; I,
your Creator, who love you dearly say
to you: freedom is to be found in
My Spirit thrice Holy; My Song of Love
to you is My gift to give you more
understanding and to draw you towards
Me, so that you will get to know
Me as your Father; blessed of My Heart,
remain true to Me, and you will
live; who desires Me? let him come to
Me and I shall be his delight as he
too will be My delight; My garden,

22

and My heaven; be blessed all you
who came in My Name in this gathering,
and be one in Our Oneness ♡

A ☧ Ω

(Someone made a video tape while I was reading it out to the assembly. Then one of
the members wanted to watch the
video once more, in the camera. He saw
that the icon of the Pantocrator that
was on the table near me, was
simultaneously moving His lips while I
was reading out the message. His
lips were synchronized with mine.)

                    Japan   23. 6. 97

My Vassula, be in peace; let us pray
to the Father:

23

Father,
in Your faithful love,
turn towards Japan,
in Your immense tenderness
  be quick in Your mercy;
listen to the poor and the
wretched; by Your saving
power raise Japan to glorify
  You; O most tender Father,
  teach them from childhood
Your Laws so that they may
proclaim Your marvels and

24

hymn to You an un-
ceasing Hymn; let this
nation become a hymn to
the Hymn, an irresistable
perfume of incense; I pray to
You, O Lord and entreat You,
that by Your Word You may
come to this nation ♡ amen

♡ yes, the Master of All has always
loved her; *

* God means, Japan.

25

.... speak My Vassula when I speak,
be My lips and glorify Me;

A ☧ Ω

(I was kept, by the Lord, five weeks
   in Japan; many small meetings
were done; even atheists came, and
Buddhists, to hear the words of God.
Three prayer groups are now starting
to follow the spirituality of True
Life in God, a Trinitarian spirituality.)

26

13. 8. 97

My Lord, You have rained on
me a downpour of blessings,
and through these, my soul
found its Home:
the Courts of Yahweh ....
there, where You provide us with
Your Goodness and where thousands
of myriads of angels dwell;
My God, Your Name is like
a Hymn that when hearing It,
my soul exults and sings
to Its rythm;

In my ignorance, Lord, do not
deprive me ever of
Your Light... Amen

* My love, I am with you always ....
taken by your misery, My Heart
could never fail you ... you have

* Jesus replies.

TRUE LIFE IN GOD

27

become the child of Our Divine Love;
you needed someone who could teach you
not only the elementary principles of
My Law and of My Grace, but the
Message of God* in its fullness; what
I have done for My Church, I have
done it to bind you all together in
love so that you, in your understanding, will get to know Us in
Our Triune Holiness; a teaching given
by Wisdom to mere children, but

* Scriptures & God's Divine Will

28

hidden from the clever and the learned; keep your mind locked in My
Mind and prosper from within, My
love; ♡ ic

Rhodos - Greece 9. 9. 97

My hope is in You alone,
my life is in Your Hands alone,
Please, stoop to me, come
and govern my soul, Lord!

I Am; flower, satisfy your thirst
with My Presence;   with all My
Heart, yes, with all My Heart I tell
you: love the One who loves you most
and who never fails you; honour

29

My Love and honour Me; grow in My
Love and in Our Oneness; Vassula,
I shall call you to write down My
Sighs later on; those Sighs that
come out from the depths of My Heart
every minute of the day; anyone
who does injury to Me does hurt
to his own soul; I do not wish to
lose any one of you; this is why My
Soul sighs with sorrow, grieving
beyond human understanding; with
Me are riches and lasting wealth

30

and I am so eager to share them
with you; oh, but so many of you
are locked in the same sleep, a
sleep of apathy! ask Me to forgive
your past ill-will, and your wrong
doings and I shall give you a pillar
of light to illumine your dreadful
night; and you, My Vassula, endure
with Me and do not allow the enemy
to deceive you to fall into weariness,
but continue to be like an echo of
My Voice, rebounding from the clefts

31

in the mountains; having tasted My
Bread,* your soul will always long
for It; My dearest soul, make every
effort to do good in your mission;
it is neither sacrifice nor night vigils,
neither bodily labours nor any praise-
worthy actions given in My honour
that makes Me delight as a soul
who comes with her heart in her
hand and offers it to Me proclaiming

* At the same time I heard "My Bread", I also
   heard " Me "

32

her love for Me, even if it sounds
like babbling .... the one who finds Me
finds life, happy the man who discovers Me and gets to know Me. I have
given you now the Bread of Life, so
that the Day you will stand in front
of My Throne, you may come with your
hands full of good fruit and offer
your offering to Us;* make Us
known to the world and remind them,
that the Word of God is alive and

* The Holy Trinity

33

active; proclaim a Resurrected Christ,
supreme in every way and above all,
and that He comes in your days to
remind you of the Hope and the Promise; *
proclaim a risen Christ, present at all
times and among you but also within you; a risen Christ, rich in
grace and esteemed more than sceptres
and thrones, and that in His Divinity
is to be found a Power, unique in
purity and unsullied, almighty and

* The renewal of the Church by the Holy Spirit.

34

most loving to man; instruct them
of the mysteries that lie within Me
but how I reveal them to the poor
in spirit and to those who approach
Me with purity of heart; all that I
will reveal will be revealed by My
Holy Spirit and then they will get
to know Us as thrice Holy in the
Holy Spirit ♡ dearest soul, cultivate
all My sayings and follow Me; I,
Jesus Christ, love you and bless you;

ΙΧΘΥΣ ><()>

35

25. 9. 97

I invoke You, my Yahweh,
my Father,
for I know that when I do, Your
Majesty would come in splendour
all the way from heaven, descending
in glory in my quarters; to see You
my God in this inaccessible glory of
Your Divine and infinite Light is
an incomprehensible splendour;
You, the Godhead, manifesting
Yourself to me and wanting to be
united with me, desiring to be
known; Only You, and You alone
can reach me, for the gap, this
ontological abyss between You and me
can be no more there; Lord, You fill
all things without being contained neither
by their limits nor by their very being;

.... While I was still invoking Yahweh's Name,
suddenly, a figure of wonder,
looking just like the Son of Man in
His glorious Transfiguration,

36

appeared to me; the Formless One took
form, what mind is able to grasp
or understand the One who encompasses
all beings? Although the vision lacked
completeness,* He made Himself be recognized, and I am conscious about it.
The Unseen God allowed Himself to be
seen to speak and listen as friend
to friend; Invisible, yet face to face;

Yahweh, the Lord of Lords, appeared to
me, vested in full splendour; His
heavenly robe shimmering and yet
colourless; glittering as though covered
by diamonds and other precious stones;

And while I was staring, bewildered and
mystified, on this enchanting vision
of grace and uncomparable beauty,
when Yahweh, delicately had emerged from
behind the clouds, doing it with such

* It was like seeing through a grey veil

37

a graceful movement, I felt my heart blossoming; His Majesty reminded me of a
bridegroom stepping out of a pavilion;
His Presence radiated a gracefulness
that even if I tried to describe it all
my life I would never manage;

His Presence at the same time radiated
love and so much sweetness and
tenderness that my soul was swept
to the ground; His beautiful
Head was leaning slightly to the right,
like those Sacred Heart statues;
    You are beautiful my God,
although I can only peer through
        a veil, I see Your hair in
dark locks reaching Your shoulders,
and Your beautiful Face the
palor of ivory is enchanting to the eye;
    Yahweh's posture was though
of someone timid, but do not mistake
me, it was not timidity but a form
of grace and majesty;

38

Oh Yahweh, You who transcend greatness and fullness, You who are the Godhead, assumed a form in an inconceivable manner to show Yourself to the unworthy one; indeed, how can language express in words, " the things that no eye has seen and no ear has heard, things beyond the mind of man ? "

Oh come and breathe over my garden* and spread Your sweetness in my heart; why, who am I to be able to contemplate Your figure? How is it possible that You, in such glory and such splendour be attracted to our misery? You dazzled me and I am bemused with Your Lordly Beauty;

* It means 'send Your Holy Spirit to me'

39

What must it be like to contemplate
You all day long in heaven with
our bare eyes?

How and where shall I find sufficient
words to describe Your Grace and Your
  Beauty? Words surpass me,
especially that slight movement
  You made, to step out from behind
the clouds; Should I invent new
words of praise to praise Your
ineffable Beauty? Human words
of praise are nothing and will never
be sufficient ever to express what
I want to express.

In Your Pure Beauty, You hold me
captive; in Your charm, You leave
me bemused and in rapture, and
  like spring You flower my heart;
with a single one of Your glances
  and my soul feels wedded
    to my Creator;

TRUE LIFE IN GOD

40

My Creator who freed me
with one single of His glances
and set me free and at large
to proclaim His wedding song;

You guard me, and while I am going
You spread   sapphires on my path,
and like the pupil of Your Eye
   You guard my soul;
I go through fire and when I
   come out of it I am unharmed;
and when torrents of insults pour on me,
like slime, from the evil one, Your
   right Hand upholds me, with
   words sweeter than honey and
more intoxicating than wine, while
You cover my head, with Your blessings,
   adorning me like a queen;

And when my oppressors joyfully
breathe hostility and calumny
all around me, Your Majesty,
like a flash of lightning

4

sends me a cherub who lifts
my soul to mount him and soar
on the wings of the wind;
then, in Your Peace and in Your
smiles, I gaze from above on those
who keep hailing my death, but
who can never reach me,
while they tremble in their fury and
rage; no, not one enemy will ever
be able to outwit my God; why,
He Himself shall crush my oppressors;

And now, I stretch out my hands to
You;
Let everyone get to know that Goodness
and Kindness is our God thrice Holy;

I am in your midst; know My little
Vassula, that the poor will receive
more from Wisdom than the rich, who

42

glory in their glory which is no glory at all; I have anointed you with My oil *, so that in this baptismal oil I can obtain victories from you for My glory but also for your own sanctification;

In Your sweetness, let me obtain mercy from You;

I, the King of Glory and your Bridegroom as well, will satisfy the poor and you will obtain mercy, and the same sweetness I have given to My Son ♡ come and

* Oil here stands symbolically for: ' Name '

43

hear Sovereignty whisper in your ear; come and write down My Words and treasure them; I am the Guardian of your soul and from My Lips you will hear no flattery but righteousness; come and lean your head on My Heart so that in that closeness you can obtain the revelation coming from the furnace* of Love, and when you will hear Me, Choice-of-My-Son, your soul will not resist to pursue the path of righteousness and

* God means His Heart

44

goodness; then you will find your joy in the end of this path ♡ have you not heard, delightful child, that I, Yahweh, your Creator, am wedded to My creation and am everyone's Spouse* ? day and night you stumble along, creation, chasing the shadows, and not even once have you ever tried to penetrate into this mystery; if so many of you are perishing, it is because hordes of you have rejected My Knowledge;

* Is. 54 : 5

45

you have forgotten My teachings ♡ I
looked at My seeds and asked Myself: "what am I to do with them"?
they are entrenched in their deceitfulness;
how am I to make this lot, who cannot tell their right hand from their
left hand, understand that I am their
Bridegroom and all I want from them
is love, not sacrifice; knowledge of My
Heart, not holocausts nor solemn festivals;"
O royal household of Mine, you have
bartered your glory for shame!

46

have you not heard that I can lower
the heavens to come down to you? have
I not lifted up My Voice enough for
your ear, creation? for how long are
you going to chase the wind? for how
long am I to see you pursuing shadows? come to Me! My Heart is like
a Lamp to your feet and from My Lips
moistened with grace and with the dew
of divinity on them, flow rivers of grace
and boundless calls of Mercy; day and
night, My loved ones, you stumble

47

along the shadows, come to Me, and
I will touch your heart so that your
perversity melts away; then in the immensity of My Love I have for you, I
will fall like dew upon you and My
Divinity will overwhelm your misery,
encompassing it to dwell permanently in
My brightness, making out of you a
vessel of light and one spirit with
Mine; ah, Vassula,* you whom I blessed
with the unction of My Name, jealousy
inflames My Heart every time your heart

* Suddenly His Divine Gaze turned and looked
                                              at me.

48

acts like dame folly and flutters away
from Mine, pursuing frills and not My
Divine power; I tell you, My loved one,
keep your Bridegroom's principles and
bind them to your heart; these will
warm your heart and will avert you
from becoming distracted from the Presence of your Bridegroom who is only
waiting to be gracious to you, Ever-so-
loved-by-Me; and if I have asked you
to disclose My wedding song* by writing,
it was because of My zealous love

* True Life in God

49

have for each soul and because I wanted
that My loved ones have enough nourishment
while they are crossing this desert.....I
have entrusted you with one talent,
to procure for Us*, the equivalent
amount; you have done well, because you have shown to Us, in
your ardour to please Us, your
faithfulness; so now have your
retreat in Us; have your retreat in
My Heart, and taste, like in former
times, the intimate delights of My Heart;

* The Holy Trinity

50

may the essence of My Love flow like a river into your heart so that all your tiny infidelities by which they raised My Eyebrow, be washed away; behold, now I am imprinting My words on you, for the salvation of so many sinners; I have come to you with gentleness, My bride, for the renewal of the mystical Body of My Son; behold now I, your Creator, am calling you, for I have espoused you to Myself, so that in Our union

51

I would have the pleasure to adorn
you with faithfulness and with ardour;
yes, on this fragile clay, I have imprinted My Name all over you since
that day when your soul called out to
Me: " Abba! " and from thereon
I have straightened your path on earth
and taught you how to delight in Me
by being ever at play in My Presence;
I know, My Vassula, how I desired
that you love Me with all your
heart and how I longed to turn

52

your whole life into a permanent
longing and thirsting for Me, your God;
I wanted to show you My Kingdom and
My nuptial chamber where, in privacy,
we could delight one another; I,
your Bridegroom, aflame with love,
would converse intimately with you,
teaching you the knowledge of holy
things; and you, cleaving yourself
firmly to My Heart, would be aspiring
grace from the breath of Omnipotence,
so that you would not cease to be;

53

no, My chosen one, our intimate union
is not like the memory of a one-day
guest; I will not cause you to trouble
your heart by withdrawing My intimate
union from you; I will take care of
your frailty, My Vassula; see, My beloved one, how I desired to draw you
to Me as a lover who draws his loved
one in privacy; I, who am the Lover
of mankind, Spouse of My creation,
wish to draw you now to Me; ... take a
retreat in Me*... why, you must have

* This He said it as an invitation but with
                                    great solemnity.

54

heard sometimes how the bridegroom longs to be alone with his bride after the wedding? I am offering you this favour, as a prelude to our feast*; yes, on that day when you responded to My Divine Will... and by opening your heart to My Call, I enriched it from Mine so that later on you would grain everywhere those treasures; those treasures

* When I was writing these words, we were the 21.11.97; — On 28.11.97, is the 12th anniversary of True Life in God.

55

are seeds* you are obtaining from Me, whereby you were to sow them in the countries I would be sending you; that day when you submitted to My Divine Will, allowing Me to govern your life, I stood affectionately in front of you, inviting you with these words: " it is impossible for a soul to love Me, the way I want her to love Me were she to keep her distance from Me;

---

* When God pronounced the word 'seeds' I saw in front of me sapphires.

56

approach Me and taste My delights;
I wish you to become intimate
with Me; if you remain far from My
embrace, you will be unable to get to
know Me;* I have, in our intimate
union and the unction of My Love
adorned you with Knowledge: Knowledge of how to find Me and get
to know Me ♡ since I have chosen
you amongst ♥ thousands, you should
not doubt any more; act in humility so that I continue to raise you

* That is the whole secret of Knowing God: intimate union.

57

up to Me....I have washed your hands
and your mouth, so that by your
hands, cleansed, they would write
My Words and keep My books, and
by your mouth I would fragrance
every nation. through My grace, I adorn*¹
your soul with the garment of My
strength but above all I, My Vassula,
adorned you with My magnificent Works
of Wisdom so that from My beloved's
lips, anointed by My Sovereignty, We*²

*¹ He used the present term as if is continuous.
*² The Holy Trinity

58

would hear praise and honour for Our Trinitarian Holiness; *¹ continue to proclaim a Resurrected Christ and fill the whole world with fruit; tell them that Christ in His Divine Love is bending down from Heaven to revive by His Presence the work of My Hands*²; with this encouraging news, hordes of nations will come to know Us in an intimate union; tell them, daughter, how We delight when We are also treated as your Holy Companion in your daily life .... speak

*¹ God reminds me of my apostolate. *² Us.

59

as My envoy and remind My people
that I, Yahweh, am alive and active,
then, go to those* sacerdotals who do not
seek Me anymore and ask them: " why
are you never asking: where is God ? "
in My Day I will pronounce My judgment against these shepherds,
who have no knowledge of Me and who
have never tasted interiourly My sweetness;
today these shepherds have exchanged
Me for something that has no value

* 'Those', means that it is obvious that it is not
'all'.

60

nor any power in it ♡ <u>to remember My</u>
<u>Presence is what they should observe</u>;
I am not observed .... how can I say:
" they are My Son's incense," when
their only fragrance is the smell of
death ? I have given you, creation,
twelve years* of ineffable favour and I did
not want to act with speed in My
wrath ; to comfort you in these years
of favour I have spoken, I have bound
up hearts that were broken and have

* Since God started this work : True Life in God ;

61

put Peace in those hearts; My Own Heart
is a Fountain of Living Water immersing,
in these years of favour, this dry land,
giving growth where dross was only to be
found; — I always wished to rank
you as My Own; in these days, I tell
you, I who am the Bridegroom of My
creation, call each one of you: My
wedded one. why those frowns and
menaces on the sweetness of My Mouth *?
unhappy little creature, remote from
knowing Me, come! I invite you to fall

* God foresees the negative reaction of certain souls.

62

into your Bridegroom's embrace and I will show you how I, Yahweh, can adorn your spirit, lavishly offering you a flow of My Divine Love so that you, in your turn return to Me this flow of Love; then, wait and see, the day I will draw you into the nuptial chamber of My Heart, like a rose that grows on the bank of a watercourse, you will blossom to declare the greatness of My Name, calling Me: "my Father;" in the nuptial

63

chamber of My Heart, your heart will
spring up with praises and as the bridegroom rejoices in his bride, so will I
rejoice in you and you in Me; My
mighty Hand will uphold you and you
would never want to part with Me
again; indeed, your spirit, enriched by
My sweetness and fullness of My Spirit,
will cry out to all nations: " beauty
and glory is to be found in our
Creator! our Hope and our Lord! "
daughter-of-My-choice, hear and write:

64

I wish you to bear witness to My Holiness
and My Divine Sweetness, be like a loud
book, a book written by the Triune
God; but for now, I want you for
Myself alone; I want to be with My
chosen one and ride the skies with you,
lifting you from the hardships of those
who hail your death daily, I wish
now to lift you from turmoil and
unrest, rivalry, jealousy and lack-of-
love; then, in your contemplation while
you will be reposing your head on My

Excerpts from Notebook 91

25 September 97 (continued from Notebook 90)...I have been clothing you with My Son, Jesus Christ's Countenance...you are My Work; p. 1.

✠ I will continue to multiply on this heart My favours and My gifts so that it can continue to sing My Hymn of Love to every nation; p. 4.

✠ Bless your persecutors...to obtain Mercy in the day of Judgment; p. 5.

✠ I have...shown you how to be intimate and at ease with Me, p. 8.

✠ I delight in souls who allow themselves to be lifted by Me...I wish to bring every soul close to My Heart; p. 11.

✠ We sent you out of Our embrace into the wilderness to defend the Truth; p. 15.

✠ What sort of honour would it have been for Me, were they (your works) to be offered without you freely giving Me your entire heart first; p. 17.

✠ What I want is love, not sacrifice;... knowledge of Myself, not holocausts; p. 17.

✠ I shall not be hard on anyone so long as I find readiness in them; p. 18.

✠ I entrusted you with this Work to enlighten this dark and apostatized world; p. 24.

✠ My Eyes were always drawn to man of humbled and contrite spirit, and I...will bring My creation to a rebirth, blessed by My Holy Spirit, as never seen before in history; p. 26.

✠ We will address Our Hymn of Love to this dying generation and whosoever listens, is blessed; whosoever listens to it will grow tall and strong too like a tree because its root will be growing in My Commandments and My decrees; p. 31.

26 October 97...Utter what I uttered to you; break the silence of death and quote My Words; make Me known to those who never sought Me; p. 38.

✠ Reflect upon, that I Am who I Am, is their Bridegroom; this is a mystery; p. 39.

NB
91

2 November 97...This Heart is your resting place;...the Unique, the Prime and the Ultimate place in which your tormented souls would find an everlasting and affectionate peace and sweetness; p. 42.

✠ Your utter wretchedness moves My Heart and My whole Being to such an extent that My Eyes fill up with tears of Mercy every time I look at you; p. 46.

✠ Do not allow your mind to wander away in the world since from the world you will receive nothing; p. 47.

✠ Always be available for Me and well-disposed; and in this way you will save both yourself and those who listen to you; p. 49.

✠ I am known to call the least of My creation; then, I looked at you and loved you; p. 51.

✠ By reposing your head on My Heart...I would be the movement of your heart, the eloquence and charm of your speech, I would be the light of your eyes to give good counsel to those who need it; p. 54.

✠ The world will always be trying to deceive you and wound the one who is so precious to Me; p. 56.

✠ When you listen to the world that takes your mind away from contemplation, this alone wounds My Heart; p. 57.

✠ When this cold world assails you...tries to disfigure your soul...run to Me; p. 57.

✠ My union with you...is so complete that you must no more lose trust; p. 58.

✠ If ever the world persists in questioning My choice, let their sins fall on their own heads; p. 61.

✠ Were you to make reparations for them, then in My Infinite Mercy I will compel them to see their sin; p. 61.

✠ My jealous love would not suffer us to ever be separated and our union broken; p. 62.

✠ My Divine Will rooted in you is the greatest gift I could offer in exchange of yours; with My Divine Will in you I could make up for all your deficiencies...the words you utter would be Mine; p. 64.

Bosom I will be augmenting in your heart My Divine teachings; you will learn to do good all the days of your life, and you will grow thus in My Heart, giving a sweet smell like the lilies; and when I would be sending you abroad to different nations you will spread your fragrance on them and it will be received like a blessing because you would be growing in My Heart; behold, I have been clothing you with My Son, Jesus Christ's

2

Countenance* so that they understand
that you are My Work, granted to them
by My Grace to be echoing Me; so continue to be My Echo, let My Words be
flowing like wine from your lips, inebriating the hearts of My sons and
daughters;

> Lord, I am and remain still
>   full of wonderment, on Your
> Beauty; in the night of my soul
> You appeared, a figure of wonder,
> like the Son of Man in His

* When so many people see Jesus appearing
in my face.

3

Transfiguration, O Triune Bridegroom, full of grace and
sovereignty, fairer than all
the angels put together,
    what does all of this signify?
By what inspiration Your Heart
    made You look at me? But I
will dare say what I wanted:
    By what folly of Your Love
    Your Heart made You look
at my wretchedness?

Most unworthy as I am, here
    You are, reminding me of
    our matrimonial bonds, draw-
ing me even deeper now in Your
    Heart to savour the delights
that lie within It so that I
can obtain the flow of Your
    Divinity and keep me alive;

daughter, if I have poured and am

4

continuing to pour out My grace on
you it is because I want your soul
to be fairer and brighter every day
that passes by until it reaches the
perfection desired by Me; I can then
say, "this heart has given Me back
all that I required and I have obtained
great victories from it; I have obtained
at the same time great pleasure from
it and through My grace, I will continue
to multiply on this heart My favours
and My gifts so that it can continue

5

to sing My Hymn of Love to every
nation;" I will continue to pour
out in your heart My delights and
consolations, like someone pouring water
from a jug into a glass, so will I
fill your heart with My Love;*

A shadow passed my thoughts,
and I was thinking again of those
who, my Lord, calumniate Your
message; with frenzy, especially Your
language of Love.
pray for those, and bless your perse-

* This image of a jug and a glass being
filled was one of the first drawings my
angel Daniel drew for me, back in 1985

True Life in God

6

cutors to be able to obtain Mercy in the day of Judgment; flesh and blood will always brood evil and take pleasure in doing evil; these same souls do not talk about My sweetness nor of My Divinity because their minds do not know how to separate My Divine sweetness from their own flesh and blood's desires; no, they do not see that there is a difference; when I speak, My dove, with My lips that are moist with grace,

7

holiness and sweetness, they do not understand My sayings and cannot fathom My purity in My Magnificence; their hearts are so hard that it becomes impossible for them to fathom the brightness and the Divinity of My Heart; this is why these hearts are eclipsed from My Light and in their perishable body and thought they accuse Me that My Words are excessive and sentimental; these are of whom I say: "they are strangers to

8

Me and they do not know Me..."
ah, My delicate soul, you have tasted
My sweetness in My Divinity and I have
procured for your soul the taste of
My Magnificence and now look at you,
look at the immensity of your thirst
for Me; I have, My bride, as a Bridegroom newly married, shown you how
to be intimate and at ease with Me,
for nothing is dark in My company;
and so many have learnt from you
and I have obtained great triumphs from

9

the grace I have given you; when
your heart is bound to Mine, there
is no darkness, but delight and joy
all the days of your life;

Yahweh, You who stepped out of
Heaven, like a bridegroom coming
out of his pavilion, have shown
me Your Face, to enjoy Your
sweetness*;

Let the gossip of the wicked hear
and learn from David's psalms
that their hostility against the
sweetness of Your language is
groundless;

Let them learn by reading Your
psalms that You are

* Ps 27:4 - - -

10

the Psalm of Your psalms,
and that Your Words, Lover
of mankind, are sweeter than
honey, even than honey that drips
from the comb; *

For this, by the mere memory of
the vision given to me in Your
immense graciousness, my soul
melts and is swept away, once more,
to the ground;

What shall I add to this? What can
one add to such a sublime vision?
But Your generosity deigned to reveal
Yourself to someone as unworthy as
myself; this was a free gift of
Your great love;

You did not need to take permission
from anyone; You wanted
to show Yourself, Your blessedness,

Ps 19 : 10

II

your charm, your radiance,
your perfect beauty and your sweetness;

Great is your Greatness and I
shall not ever forget this sweet vision
that has been imprinted in my memory;

I delight in souls who allow themselves
to be lifted by Me .... ah, Vassula, I
wish to bring every soul close to My
Heart and have it grafted on Me, in
the same way I have brought you to be
close to My Heart; this is 'why', My child,
I am tracing ever so graciously a path
so that everyone can follow it; a path

12

of righteousness that leads to Me ; for this
reason, I, as a young bridegroom in love,
am in love with My creation : the Work
of My Hands ; and I will expose to every
creature the flame of My Heart, whether
friend or foe ; today, many of you
scrutinize My Love and My sweetness,
modelling Me according to the passions of
your flesh ; I tell you : they who know
Me observe holy things holily ; these
will be adjudged one day, holy ; but
as for those who do not know Me and

13

do not observe holy things holily, they will be adjudged as they merit it. ♡ My Heart is pulsating with calls of love to love, and again I say: whether friend or foe you are all invited to partake the delights of My Heart and when you do, you will realize how you belittled Me all your life, how you belittled My Magnificence by your very weak nature and your worldly inclinations and by having believed that your exterior pleasures and delights, desired by your

14

flesh, were lordly and great; these delights and pleasures of your flesh can never be measured with My Divinity and sweetness ♡ your delights to Mine are like a grain of sand in the universe when compared to the bliss you can obtain from My sweet- ness that would lead you to eternal joy; and you, Vassula, you who have entered into the delights of Our Trinitarian Holiness and have come to understand Our tender affection and Our infinite Love, We rejoice for having accepted voluntarily

15

to lay Our Work upon you, hence
becoming a living altar, increasing Our joy;
We have converted you and led you to
contemplate a Spousal contemplation in
the intimate union of Our Oneness; then,
We sent you out of Our embrace into the
wilderness to defend the Truth; but now
after your hard labours, We want you
to repose on Our Heart and have the
leisure of contemplating Our Trinitarian Holiness; in this intent repose you will be
suckled by Our Divinity; today again

16

I offer you My Heart and as a bridegroom who steps out from his pavilion to join his bride, I, stepped out to join My Heart to yours and take My pleasure in you, and exchange in our caresses our mutual love; let it be as in heaven:

Love for love,

Heart for heart;

yes! you have not refused to acknowledge Me as Father, in My Triune Holiness; and like a vessel that carries water, your heart, after acknowledging Me, was

17

filled with My Living Water to bring it
to perfect the virtues I would be offering
it ♡ My Works would be sterile were
I ♡ not to perfect you in your love; of what
use would have been your works to Me,
and what sort of honour would it have
been for Me, were they to be offered without you freely giving Me your entire heart
first; indeed, come and learn the meaning of these words: "what I want is
love, not sacrifice; what I want is
knowledge of Myself, not holocausts;"

18

I shall not be hard on anyone so long as I find readiness in them; have you not heard: " a man is acceptable with whatever he can afford; " so, you who read Me and are My Work too, come to Me, as you are, and I, in My perfect Love, will perfect you; I shall ravish your heart so that I may obtain from it the rarest and the most delicate fragrances; then like someone stretching upwards his hands holding a golden bowl full of incense, to perfume My Holiness, I will lift your

19

heart, holding it upwards, letting those rarest essences swirl out on the earth, spreading your sweet fragrance all around Me, delighting Me, and delighting all the saints and angels in heaven; My joy will be such that it will be taken as a wedding dance*; while My angels' mouths will be filled with laughter and their lips with song;   and I, exulted with joy, in your nothingness, I would turn your

---

* I had seen in a vision, Yahweh our Lord, holding in His outstretched Hands this 'bowl' and going around, swaying like in a dance.

20

heart into a jewel, and with My Hands still outstretched, lifting your heart, I would anoint you, My jewel, and bless you; and like I had once placed you with tenderness into your mother's womb to be nourished and to grow, I will place you in My Heart to nourish your soul with My Divinity, allowing you to grow with My Holiness ♡ this will be the proof of My Love to you; and you will get to know Yahweh, your Bride-groom, thrice Holy, as never before;

21

then, your soul will be cleaved so pro-
foundly on My Heart and in Me, that
you will never forget Me because your
soul would have fallen voluntarily captive
to My charms ♡ and I, who only act
out of love, will fasten your little
heart on integrity, willingness and love,
and enflame it with divine fire; I will
make you taste My sweetness by having
you share with My Son Jesus, the One
nearest to My Heart, Our Blessedness,
inviting you to enter into the True

22

and Unique Knowledge of Our Triune
Deity; this Knowledge of Ourselves will
teach you that We can give you back
your divinity, divinizing your soul to enter
into Eternal Life ♡ and that Our Divine
Light can glitter too into your soul and
body to live in Our Light and in Us;
then, My beloved one, I will enrich your
soul with graciousness, and while I will
be hiding you in My Heart, I will take
away your sins, so that you move in the
Spirit and breathe the inspirations of

23

My Heart, while I will be engraving
you with the seal of consecration,
anointing you with My Holy Name;
then, you will no longer belong to
yourself but to the One who moves you
in union in Our Oneness ♡ I, the
Most High, Bridegroom of ♡ My creation,
will show you such fullness of love
and tenderness that your soul will
taste what it is like in heaven
while you would still be on earth;
My sweetness will be such that you

24

would be as though inebriated with wine, because you would be tasting the Almighty's Love, this Love which would be like a paradise of blessing and which will adorn your soul with more than glory; — feel the greatness of My Love, Vassula; I have chosen you out of all the living and made a lily out of you, allowing you to hear My Voice; I entrusted you with this Work to enlighten this dark and apostatized world; I have sent you out

25

to fragrance with My Work the wilderness of My creation and shine upon
them My decrees and My Law, and
the world, one day, would see in
you My supreme power and would say:
"truly, God is hidden with you,"
but they would be saying it to your
departed spirit; yes!* you are, indeed,
a true witness of the Most High, because I have made your mouth a sharp

---

* This "yes!" came like the sound of thunder-
bolt, it was said with such power & authority.

26

sword ♡ ♡

My God! sometimes I feel I am
hemmed in by my oppressors, even
during the night I see the fangs of
those who would want to devour me,
fabricating falsehood to see me
condemned, O help me against
the proud! For how long will
you keep their eyes shut?

until your Service to Me would be
completed and the Ceremony would come
to its end; — My Eyes were always
drawn to man of humbled and contrite
spirit, and I, who am known to bring
to birth, I will bring My creation

27

to a rebirth, blessed by My Holy Spirit, as never seen before in history; My Flame within My Heart will be your purification, creation, and this will be executing My judgement*; this will be done so as to remove your veil and see Me clothed in glorious beauty and holiness; I will be executing My act of love* so that I win you to Myself ♡ then you, in your turn, will turn to Me; you too will become a witness

* small judgement.

TRUE LIFE IN GOD

28

of My Love; and when people, surprised with your change of heart will ask you the reason for your humble behaviour, you will reply : " I have learnt from my Father; I have listened to my Spouse and so I have become a son of light ; my God is my Light, and eternal life is that we should know Him as the only True God and So-vereign of all creation; then, my friends, you too will belong to the Spouse for ever and ever; " ah,

29

generation, have you not heard My
Son, Jesus Christ say to you :
    " the hour will come - in fact it
is already here - when the dead *¹ will
hear the Voice of the Son of God
and all who hear it will live; for
the Father who is the source of life
has made the Son the source of life"²;
so why are you afraid in these evil
times of the profusion of Our Riches of
Our Heart, poured out on you?

* ¹ The spiritual dead.
*² Jn 5: 25-26

30

why are you astounded at My marvels of today? are We not the Source of Life? the mountains totter with the smell of death that rises from My creation and the waters roar and seethe in agony when they hear My agony when I see My Own seed dying together with this world that disintegrates in sin and wickedness; should We then bind Our Mouth? We are the Source of Life and from this Source, Our Heart stirs yours with

31

Our Noble Theme: We will address
Our Hymn of Love to this dying
generation and whosoever listens, _is_
blessed ♡ whosoever listens to it will
grow tall and strong too like a tree
because its root will be growing in My
Commandments and My decrees; —
not long ago, I planted a seedling *
today it grew into a tree and its top
reached the sky, tasting now and
then the essences and the fragrant
breeze of heaven; now it is known

* Yahweh, I understood, speaks of me and this Message

32

in every nation, since it is seen from
the ends of the earth and from every
direction; its green foliage is medicinal
and as a healing balm for the sick,
but at the same time an appeasing
fragrance to the poor and the wretched;
I have been blowing kisses to it to
increase its fruit and perfect it; in
its beauty its fruit, abundant, is
marked with the Seal of My Holy
Spirit; every nation, no matter
what race and from where they

33

come can reach it and have
their fill from it; its produce is enough
for all; even to the unworthy this
tree can provide shade and comfort;
I am its Keeper; I have seen, so many
times, men creeping and slithering by
night, with fire in their hand, to
put alight My tree and destroy it, but
since I had foreseen all of this, to
protect it, I had gathered armies of
My Angels, long before this happens,
to have it drenched with the dew of

34

heaven; I have swept away My enemies
as you have seen; so do not say, My
beloved: "but will not the eagle
break my root and snap up my
fruit so that all the new leaves will
wither in one go when they shoot?"
no!* no, My tree, I tell you, you will
keep growing and will continue to bear
fruit with the Seal and fragrance
of My Holy Spirit; I shall multiply
your foliage and your fruit so
that it will be enough for all

* The way He said "no" brought me tears in my eyes

35

and for every new generation to come....

Lord, my heart lives for You
and my spirit sings praises
all day long for You;

It is you who have kept my soul
hidden in Your Heart and You
who protect me;

Although there is an ontological
abyss between You and me, I am
within You in Your Majesty, and
You, without losing Your transcendence,
You are within me;

Vassula, many trees will be cut down
and some I will uproot altogether and
have their root burnt; that Day
the foundations of the earth will

36

shake with the sound of My Voice,
and My House will be filled with My
cry :   " enough! enough now! "

> May you show kindness and bless us,
> and make Your Face smile on us!
> For then the earth will acknowledge
> Your ways,
> and all the nations will know of
> Your power to save;
>
> Ps. 67 : 1-2

flower of My Heart, such words are
the delight of your Bridegroom; come
now and listen to the pulsations of
My Heart !

АΩ

37

(This previous message although it is dated
25.9.97, has ended on the 25.10.97;
it was given to me now and then, when
I was called.)

26.10.97

Lord, Father and Master of my life,
do not let temptation grip me to doubt;
there is in my heart a desire that,
blazing like a furnace, cannot be
quenched until it is slaked; the
desire of drawing souls to You,
but temptation grips me to doubt
that You have indeed opened my
mouth and raised me up in
Your Courts;

I am your Fortitude; senseless little
child, have you not understood? I am
the One who fills you with My Know-

38

ledge; I am the Holy One who fills your heart with joy; it is I, your Father; never mind about your bewilderment ♡ pray with your heart to Me; trust Me and allow yourself to be immersed in the Ocean of My Mercy; satisfy My thirst for souls. Goodness and Mercy are a light to your feet; I have manifested My Love to you so that you understand Me; be like a loud book and speak, utter what I uttered to you;

39

break the silence of death and quote My Words; make Me known to those who never sought Me, to reflect upon that I Am who I Am, is their Bridegroom; this is a mystery defying not only the apostates but also all those who, although they preach My Word, have never met Me and do not know Me; I, your Lord, Father, Bridegroom and Master of your life, bless you in Our Trinitarian Holiness; see? in My Name too, bless

40

My people;

A ☧ Ω

Sunday -　　2. 11. 97

While I was in the Greek Orthodox Church, attending Mass, suddenly a fear gripped me and thought that I might be indisposed to receive Our Good Lord in the Holy Communion, and that if that was the sose, I might cause to bring forth upon me, with wrath, the Judgement of God.

While those thoughts were crossing back and forth in my mind, I experienced suddenly, in my heart a joy and delight, that even though they came out first from my heart, these seemed to spread like a warm soothing liquid inside my very bones; while I was experiencing this consolation, my soul was being transformed to come out

41

of its fear and gloom, into delights
and light;   in this joy, my
soul praised the Lord and I sung
to Him in silence. I revived.

Then, all of a sudden I saw our
Lord open His Mouth to say something
to me; I could not help notice
how cheerful He was and with
delight He said to me:

come to Me ....

While opening at the same time His
greenish-blue mantle. This gesture of
His attracted me as an iron is
attracted and drawn to a magnet; in
this same manner my soul was
drawn irresistably to His Heart;

And I found my head leaning on His
Bosom. Then, ever so tenderly,
the Lover of mankind said to me:

42

ah, how utterly wretched you could be!

I was thinking, ' can someone hug fire to their breast without setting their bosom alight?` Here I am, hugging the Sacred Heart, how can my own heart not catch the ' fire of love '?

While I had leaned my head on His Divine Heart and while I was still leaning on His Bosom, I felt His Bosom melting away and my head being absorbed into His Body; my head went through Him and through His Sacred Heart, and I found my head encompassed in His Heart resting in this way on the Son who is nearest to the Father's Heart.

this Heart <u>is</u> your resting place; vessel-of-My-Light, this Heart is the

43

Unique, the Prime and the Ultimate place in which your tormented souls would find an everlasting and affectionate peace and sweetness;

While my Beloved was saying these sweet words to me, He put His Arms around me, tightening them on me, pressing me now even more on His Bosom and as though one who wants to protect someone from being cold, He hid me completely in His Mantle;

This form of holding me was as one who is afraid to lose the one he holds.

I was considering, while I was having this experience, in the Church, whether I should write it down or not,

44

and He said:

write it for the benefit of souls and
I will join too while you are writing,
to write down My part ♡

The Lord's Heart by now absorbed
entirely my head. It was like a
gateway to Heaven and during those
delightful moments while my soul
was enjoying this ineffable sweetness
and tenderness of this heavenly repose,
    my head was being constantly
covered by caresses.

I have lavished your soul with My
favours; I ask you now to remain in
My Heart in this way; remain with

45

Me, My beloved one;

Then, while my soul felt inebriated
as though with wine, the Lord made
me taste in His Heart the sweetness
of Himself, reminding me of the sweet
taste of our Holy Communion* and
at the same time my head was
being covered by a sweet fragrance,
again, like the Holy Communion;

Then, while I was still in that
repose, I noticed my surroundings
being filled with smoke, the
sweet smoke of burnt incense. In
this serene surrounding I kept hearing
my Lord and my Beloved repeat
those words:

remain here, remain in Me, then come

* The Orthodox H. Communion

46

foreward and receive Me; delight Me and remain in here;

I sighed and wondered what makes Our Lord delight so much on a creature such as me. The zero of the zeroes. He, the Perfect Being, He who suffices by Himself, how was it possible to even imagine He would look at me twice?

your utter wretchedness moves My Heart and My whole Being to such an extent that My Eyes fill up with tears of Mercy every time I look at you ♡

I was about to say something ....

47

no; do not speak; absorb My Peace
and satisfy your heart in this silence,
enjoy these moments of grace and absorb the sweetness your Lord is offering
you; refresh your heart, My loved one,
and remain in My embrace and allow
yourself to be loved; do not allow your
mind to wander away in the world since
from the world you will receive nothing;
come to Me and taste My sweet love
I have for you and always had

48

for you; *   — say : an ineffable weakness for you, instead ♡ dearest gem in My Hand, the unction of My Love for you is so great that in those enflamed moments of love, My Divine Eyes cannot be but transfixed on you; think hard about this, until I arrive to fetch you; I find no other pleasure elsewhere than in those moments when I am

---

* While Our Lord and my Divine Master was saying these words, it seemed as though honey was dripping from His Mouth. And I understood that He had a special weakness for me, from the beginning of my life.

49

with you and you are like an open book to Me, to write in you My New Hymn of Love; always be available for Me and well-disposed, and in this way you will save both yourself and those who listen to you; I formed you to become My pupil;

Lord! when I think of it, You formed me in a most amazing way; You formed me in silence through Your Holy Spirit and by breathing in me those divine revelations from Your Sacred Heart! It was not like when You formed audibly Your disciples!

50

yes! I wanted you turn to Me wholeheartedly so that I would draw your
heart towards My Love and My Fortitude ♡ I wanted to prepare your soul
to carry My Divine Message; ah Vassula, all that I say to you now,
you will hear again when I will appear
to you openly at the appointed time;
now My Soul rejoices in looking at
My garden* and I enjoy breathing in
you; every step you allow Me to

* my soul

51

take in My garden, will be done with gentleness and it will be consoling for you;

When Your Divine Gaze turned down on earth to ravish my heart, how was it possible that by only looking at me You did not flee, but instead, my unworthiness gave You so much joy, attracting You to me?

I am known to call the least of My creation; then, I looked at you and loved you ∴... I told you in the beginning that,

* The words of His Mouth were like honey; it is He, my Friend, to whom sweet conversation bound me in His Heart.

52

were you to let Me form you, I would lead you with strings of love by My grace, imprinting on your soul My Divine Image, and with this Divine Seal which is the imprint of the Holy Trinity, you would be drawn into the fullness of Our Deity, perfecting thus your intimate union with Us in Our Divine Love; I still intend, dearest one, to continue and whisper in your ear My secret revelations and while I will be pouring on you abundantly My gifts and My

53

favours for My good pleasure, I will keep reminding you that by having drawn your heart so inseparably into Mine, it was so that in this courteous gesture of Mine, our union would be complete and that your spirit, through My grace, would become one with Me;* I had given you a prayer*² in which you consecrate body and soul to My Sacred Heart, so that your thoughts would be My thoughts, your acts My acts, giving Me voluntarily your will so that My

* 1 Co 6:17   *² Consecration of 26.1.92

54

Will be done in you; I remind you that by reposing your head on My Heart, in these moments of interiour enjoyment, I would be the movement of your heart, the eloquence and charm of your speech, I would be the light of your eyes to give good counsel to those who need it; every movement of yours, every gesture would be coming from Me; you would be listening to all of My sighs, understanding* their meaning so that you would be acting according to My Divine Will; through grace

* I heard at the same time the word, "decoding."

55

you will be inhaling My sweetness as you did when your head was resting on My Heart tasting Its sweet savours[*]; remember how My Father instructed you[*2]? He told you that were you to allow Him to strengthen the bonds of union with Him, your soul then would be so joined to Him and your spirit so englobed in Mine that everything you would be doing would be according to My Mind; your works would be rooted in Our Goodness and your

[*] My vision in Church   [*2] Message of 16.3.87

TRUE LIFE IN GOD

56

performance in Our Spirit; then My Father gave you an example of the way the members of your body work : " you just do not tell your hand what to do, but it works with your will." this would be the manner in which We would be guiding you;

Lord, forgive my lack of confidence towards You, and to all these abundant graces You have given to me freely in my utter unworthiness. I was hiding Your graces; I have sinned from fear of what others think;

the world will always be trying to deceive you and wound the one who is

57

so precious to Me; and when you listen
to the world that takes your mind away
from contemplation, this alone wounds
My Heart*; by grace I have drawn you
into My Sacred Heart so that you be
Mine alone and by grace I intend to
keep you in this repose; when this cold
world assails you with its temptations,

* I understood that by hiding the graces of
our Lord and even not quite admitting these
under the pretext of my unworthiness, Jesus
becomes quite upset and sad.

58

and tries to disfigure your soul to resemble them, run to Me and take your refuge in My Heart; have confidence in Me and confide in Me all your problems; I am only waiting to be gracious to you, My chosen one; the world would always try to draw you back into its entrails, a dark valley where there is only desolation; but I have chosen you amongst thousands, so why do you sadden Me with your lack of confidence? My union with you in the Light of My

59

Divinity is so complete that you must no more lose trust but place your head on My Heart and doubt no longer on our blessed union; come and say to Me now: " my Jesus, Divine Mercy, I lacked confidence in You and so I have brought Your Heart to distress; I now ask You in my bareness and in all humility to be forgiven so that You may, in Your Infinite Mercy and Goodness, restore my disfigured

60

and wounded soul; disfigured
and wounded by the world's acts
upon me and their sayings " *
I have received your prayer with delight;
in your deficiencies, I will make up to
glorify My Name thrice Holy; from
now on do not let Me ever fall

* (I said it.) I realized how the evil
one was invariably trying to impress
on me through the mouth of the world
that this Work, so Divine of God,
was less important than its real value,
thus under-estimating its value, and
always trying to diminish its importance. I would
find myself in a constant battle, trying to keep
away these false accusations, and never giving in
to them.

61

into any distress or sorrow that leave all
My saints and angels in immense distress
for being unable to relieve My pain;
if ever the world persists in questioning
My choice, let their sins fall on
their own heads; it is with justice that I
will intervene; if they treat My chosen
one as they please, the one My Sacred
Heart regards with particular affection,
I will reprove them mightily* but were
you to make reparations for them, then
in My Infinite Mercy I will compel

* Then He looked at me.

62

them to see their sin; I have in My
love, as I have told you in the
beginning, bonded you to Me in such
a way that it would be difficult for
you to loosen these bonds*; I performed
this act, after your 'fiat' to Me, out of
pure love; My jealous love would not
suffer us to ever be separated and
our union broken; I have in a moment of inebriated delight, given you a
further grace : a matrimonial union
thus drawing you even deeper into

* _Message of 16.3.87_

63

the repose of a sweet contemplation in My Divine Heart; in this delightful union between you and the Holy Trinity you would become Our Harp, and We would use you with delight obtaining great triumphs from you; then you, in your turn would enjoy sharing with Us Our Courts; in Our Divine Grace you would become Our Litany;* lily of My Heart, Infinite Tenderness was shown to you so that others would learn from you and obtain the same

* For my life would become a ceaseless prayer.

64

quantity as you have obtained; lily of
My Heart, Our closeness to you is your
blessedness; My Divine Will rooted in
you is the greatest gift I could offer
in exchange of yours; with My Divine
Will in you I could make up for all
you deficiencies and your insufficiencies;
the words you utter would be Mine
because I would be your vestment
and you would have My Mind; although
you are oftened blamed for your severity, in reality your severity is not

Excerpts from Notebook 92

2 November 97 (continued from Notebook 91)...A soul once united to God becomes one spirit and one mind with Him; p. 1.

✠ Others would imply that My honourable gifts...are not divine...I have given them enough proof and I shall give no more proof; p. 4.

✠ So long as your head would be resting on My Heart...you would be able to give good counsel to those who need it; p. 6.

✠ Do not worry anymore, I will continue to look after your various needs;...I will always come and bring you back from any hazardous paths you might be tempted to take; p. 7.

✠ I have given you Messages of extreme gravity;...My Spirit has been and is your Guide and your Light; p. 9.

✠ May the heart of the reader who has read these pages, open! may his eyes and ears, open! p. 15.

✠ You still have not penetrated into what is beyond all price, and what I have been offering you...the tremendous grace of knowing Me in an intimate union; p. 15.

✠ Many of you are busy with your daily chores, which please Me if they are done with love and...according to My Mind, but this would be incomplete if you do not open to grace and acknowledge Me; p. 17.

NB 92

17 December 97...I want, My Vassula, for this generation and for the generations to come, to leave an everlasting memory of My Mercy; p. 22.

✠ Since I am the Lord of the saints, I am no less Lord than of the wretched;...I am renowned for My Mercy; p. 23.

✠ To call such a wretched soul...is a sign you should not ignore, it is a sign for the rest of you to...learn that I call every soul...to turn to Me; p. 28.

22 January 98 (India)...May this whole nation...marvel at My deeds and be filled with my graciousness; p. 29.

✠ Come to Me with prayers...for the conversion of the world;...this is My Grace passing now on you; be one in My Name...what I need is love, reconciliation and a spirit of forgiveness; p. 32.

25 February 98...I have entrusted you with the noblest of My Works in your times; this Divine Work is placed in your hands; p. 37.

✠ A true life in Me, is to be living the same kind of life as Christ lived;...tell Me, of what use is a fruit-tree which would never produce its fruit? or...a harp without its strings? p. 40.

✠ You who were created for Our Imperial Courts, would be according to My Mind in all its aspects; I will sanctify you, and you will receive the power to become wholly devout; p. 47.

✠ Today when My Voice is audible, It frightens them out of their minds and immediately do everything in their power to subdue It; p. 49.

✠ I am about to open the heavens and let you know the mystery of My purpose: the outpouring of My Holy Spirit, Who is the Promise written in Scriptures and Who was to act upon My creation like never before in history, p. 49.

✠ I am about to shatter into smithereens, with the power and the grace of My Holy Spirit, the barriers of your division and unite you, for My honour, in a single Body; p. 50.

✠ I will adorn this earth in Spring; My Spring;...when the whole of My creation will be shining with a brilliant light; in the baptism of the Purification you will be reformed into your first image; p. 53.

✠ Love is on the way of return to restore His Kingdom; this will be the reign of My Kingdom on earth and My Will shall be done on earth as it is in heaven; p. 54.

✠ So now is the time of repentance; this is a wicked age but your lives should redeem it; renounce your will and find favor with me by recognizing what is My will; p. 55.

✠ We put to you the duty of passing on Our divine Word to many nations and so you have done what you were asked to do; p. 61.

yours but Mine; those that reproached
you for this have not quite renounced
their sin .... they keep forgetting that a
soul once united to God becomes one
spirit and one mind with Him; I have
granted you for your mission all these
gifts out of the Love I have for you,
but also for the restoration of My House;
ah Vassula, some would ask: " why
is the Lord emphasizing His union,
His gifts and graces so much ? " if I
am reminding you all of these things,

2

it is because the world will keep trying
to compel My chosen one to doubt of
My gifts given to her; I had, My
Vassula, warned you in the early days
of your mission that your acts of
love would be misunderstood and
that you would be hounded like game
and that you would suffer adversity,
but also how My fatherly protection
would always cover you, and I would
come to your rescue to console you and
lift you from the fangs of the evil one;

3

I had told you that My royal Messages
would be so often spat upon, rejected
and ridiculed, but also how I would
always stand by you to encourage you;
you are still dwelling on earth but I
am dwelling well within you; so do
not fear. so long as you are on earth,
the world, in its darkness will keep
trying to harm you and injure you; I
do not mean that you should part
from your friends, but remember,
do not trust yourself to people;* some

* Jn 2 : 24

4

would want to force your hand to do
what is contrary to your wishes, which would
also be contrary to My Own wishes ♡ others
would imply that My honourable gifts
given to you, as well as My favours, are
not divine and do not come from Me;
for these I have something to say : " if
you say they are not of divine origin
than they could only be, according
to your insinuation, from the father
of lies , or from the subconscious;
has it never occured to you that

5

by judging My Work as evil you are
sinning against the Holy Spirit and such
a sin is not forgiven? if you say that
this whole divine Work comes from the
subconscious, then explain to Me the
mastery and learnings of these writings
from someone who had no knowledge
of Wisdom's Works and had no train-
ing in even an elementary catechism;"
so far* I have given them enough proof,
and I shall give no more proof than
what I have already given; then there

* Our Lord turned and looked at me.

6

will be those who, in spite of having
asked for your advice, will ignore it,
because their soul would be still stri-
ving for their personal desires and will
submit to their human will and not
to Mine; I had told you that so long
as your head would be resting on
My Heart, you would, in these moments
of repose, be reading the pulsations of My
Heart, then you in your turn, you would be
able to give good counsel to those who
need it; but again, the world, not

7

yet overcome from its evil thoughts, would underestimate My treasures poured out on you, under the pretext that you are not confirmed*.... overcome now your lack of confidence in the gifts and favours I so generously offered you and with all your heart repeat the prayer I have given you .... (I did.) do not worry anymore, I will continue to look after your various needs;

* That the work of True Life in God is not yet approved by the Church.

8

I have prayed, Lord, but how could I be
sure I will not fail You again?

I am here to remind you; I will always
come and bring you back from any
hazardous paths you might be tempted
to take. I will keep showing you My
most delicate care I have for My
chosen ones; come, today I want you to
feel happy, because I can say in all
truth: you have made My Word
your home and you have become My
pupil and indeed Mine;

9

My God, You have enticed my
unworthy soul to follow You, and
You conferred on me valuable
riches undeservedly and in an unbounded Love You lifted up
my soul;

I lifted up your soul for the benefit
of My Church as well; Vassiliki, I
have given you Messages of extreme gravity;
I have, during all these years breathed
in you Divine revelations coming all from
My Sacred Heart; My Spirit has been and
is your Guide and your Light; I have
truly poured out on you divine graces

10

so that people can benefit from them too; all My Works are good, and they are warmly welcomed by the pure in heart and the lowly, but praise is unseemly in a sinner's mouth for My Works! I have, as I said, given you all enough proof by this Divine Treasure coming from My Sacred Heart's treasury so that you do not doubt; apart, Vassula, from having given you exterior signs of My Love, I have given you Knowledge and Instruction constantly enriching you and others through

11

these writings; are you, My dove, aware
of all those Divine inspirations breathed
in you of My Holy Spirit?

(I sighed, and felt so touched by the
tenderness of His Voice that I
find no words to describe it.)

here I am today with you, to help you
overcome all your weaknesses; I could no
longer bear to see you concealing in
your modesty My Divine gifts that I
have given you;

In Your extreme Goodness You have
deigned to give us sufficient Manna
in which our soul today rejoices;

12

It is immaterial but once one's soul
absorbs it, it hungers for more
and so, here I am, imperfect still,
and only wishing to make reparations
for the cause I gave You to bring
Your Divine Heart to distress;

Let my defects and my negligences
which caused Your sorrow be
turned into fervour, trust,
and a bunch of myrrh.

precious one, I am not insensitive to all
the hard labours of love you undertook
in My Name, nor of the hardships borne
with patience for My Sake, My dove;
I am not insensitive either to your
requests of now, and I am glad you

13

rely on My Grace;

It makes me happy to suffer for you;
do not weary on the way with Me;

Give me my Lord opportunities to open
my mouth to glorify you without fear
and without doubt.

this is why you must rely on Me and
resource your spirit from My Spirit so
that you can go on singing and chanting My Love Hymn to the nations;
this is why I invited you to have your
pilgrimage and your retreat in My
Body, My loyal helper;

14

enjoy yourself in My grace and delight in My company in this intimate light of grace given to you by My Father, and accept by tasting, as you have, the sweet savours of My Heart;

> While my Lord was saying these words, I still felt my head being encompassed in His Heart, savouring and inhaling again an essence that resembled the Holy Communion.

Suddenly it was as though Jesus turned His Holy Face away and looked at the reader. (The one who is reading these lines.) His Face was solemn, His penetrating Eyes glued on the reader. Then, while embracing me with His Arms round me, His Mantle covering me

15

completely, giving the impression of
someone protecting a victim from any
further aggression, He said:

may the heart of the reader who has

read these pages, open! may his eyes

and ears, open! up to the present time

you have not grasped entirely My Heavenly

Treasure, nor have you appreciated com-

pletely My gift* to you; you still have

not penetrated into what is beyond all

price, and what I have been offering

---

* Messages of 10.1 87 p. 23+28, 25.1.87 p. 41, 31.1.87 p. 69
in the book " My Angel Daniel. — The Father speaks:
" I will send you to all mankind; I will give you to
them as my gift, thus enabling them to understand Me
more, for this is My Will."

16

you all the days of your life :
   the tremendous grace of knowing Me
 in an intimate union and tasting
interiourly, in the nuptial chamber
of My Heart, My sweetness and My
 Divine kisses; happy those who listen to Me and obtain this grace; woe to
those who in their wretched condition and
in their stained mind resist this grace;
they shall weep in their misery one day;
it is good to do good works for Me
and follow some devotions as well as

17

acts of love, thanksgivings and acts of reparation, but I would be greatly disappointed that you would die before having known Me*[1]; I would be greatly distressed were you to die now before having understood Me*[2]; many of you are busy with your daily chores, which please Me if they are done with love and they are according to My Mind, but all of this would be incomplete if you do not

*[1] Mt 7 : 21-23 — *[2] Jr 9 : 23

18

open to grace and acknowledge Me in My
intimacy; so come and accept My familiar
companionship and I, in My good pleasure, I will take you into the mysteries
and the hidden secrets of Our Heart *'; you
and We, will become inseparably united in
Our Love for ever and ever;

(Jesus then turned to me and with a
grave look in His Eyes said:)

now I have, like in former times, spoken
to you from My Heart, to remind you,

*' The Holy Trinity

19

My child, of My Infinite Love, and especially to take away that seed that was thrust in you by the world; I could not bear any longer to see My adopted one, My joyful messenger, being shred to pieces by the misgivings the world tried to put into her mind * : your fear of My having thrust an ice-cube in your heart instead of My Divine grace, Vassula, belittles Me and has no foundation in the Truth....

* Remarks like : True Life in God messages are one thing but the messenger is completely another thing; like the 2 do not go together. Jesus is against this theory.

20

adversities have not made you lose the
Peace I have given you in your heart, and
that is good; but for My Sake, My dove,
do not ever again doubt of My graces
and unbounded Love I have for you
always; do not lose your trust in Me;
why, can you not see how divinely enamoured to folly, I am of you? so
I beg of you to trust Me; so long as
you are still on earth, remain in Me
to perfect your union with Me and
receive Me as often as you can in

21

Holy Communion, magnifying your love on Me, and abandoning yourself to Me; remain in this Resting Place* for ever, allowing Me to keep you in this Furnace of Love, to make you taste the sweetness of My Love*²

ΙΧΘΥΣ >°<

17. 12. 97

All flesh must come to You
with all its sins;
though our faults overpower us,
You blot them out.
Happy the man You choose, whom You
invite to live in Your Courts.

*¹ The Sacred Heart.   *² Ps 90: 17

22

Fill us with good things of Your house,
of Your Holy Temple.

Ps 65 : 3-4

My Vassula, let Me use your ear, so that
you hear Me; let Me use your hand
so that you write down My sayings;
then let Me use your mind to fill it
with My Knowledge and fill your whole
being with the instructions coming from
Wisdom; accept all My offers, My beloved
friend, and you will advance in the
pace I had foreseen; I want, My Vassula, for this generation and for the

23

generations to come, to leave an everlasting memory of My Mercy; none of all
these Riches that are coming from the
treasury of My Heart would be attributed
to you, since you knew nothing at all
in the beginning at the time when you
were called by the Lover of mankind, since
your whole body laid then in darkness;
but since I am the Lord of the saints,
I am no less Lord than of the wretched;
I looked at you and loved you I
am renowned for My Mercy and for the

24

tenderness of My Heart; I am renowned for
the weakness I have for children; rejoice
then, daughter, that your King stooped
from His Throne to give you thrice
the kisses of resurrection on your soul;
inebriated by the sweetness of My kisses, your
soul now sings praises to Me, glorifying
your Lover; I knew then that by
throwing just one of My glances on you
I would soften instantly the hardness of
your self-will and shatter the crust
surrounding your heart; and so I did....

25

oh, what would I not do for such a frail soul to bring it to a complete spiritual union with My Deity and make it one spirit with Me! I have bidden you, My beloved, to build a holy temple within you, an altar in the city where We* would pitch Our tent, a copy of that sacred tabernacle which We had prepared from the beginning, and so you have, faithful little friend; this is why Wisdom was able to help you and through

* The Holy Trinity

26

you thousands of other souls; Wisdom
educated you and many others through
this Divine Work, leading everyone into a
marvelous road; this Work is the proof
of My overflowing Love;

O blessed and overflowing with graces
    Heart of Jesus, Divine Goodness,
you who with one of Your glances
overthrow kings and kingdoms, intoxicating cities and towns, inebriating
to folly hearts and holding them
captives of love and for ever enamoured of Your Divinity,

Your Eyes my Lord are a Garden
    of Eden, Exquisitely beautiful;

27

Your Heart is like an infinite
universe of grace in Grace,
your whole being, like an ivory
tower with glittering precious
stones encrusted on its walls;

Eternal Light, Your two Natures are
the movement of our heart;

O God! I find that I do not suffice
to form one intelligible word that
might come close enough to describe
such Sovereignty and Splendour as
this of my Lord's.

ah Vassula, My comfort! I was determi-
ned to take you to share My Kingdom!
this Love I have, this thirst I have for
souls, burns in My Heart; it is love

28

that led Me to the Cross, unmindful of its shamefulness; it is My Love that leads Me now to you, generation, calling one of the most inadequate creatures amongst you, the one who lacked the knowledge not only of Scriptures but also the knowledge of My Will; at that time, a scandal in the eyes of My saints and angels; to call such a wretched soul from her death and raise her to My Divine Heart, bringing her up in My royal courts, is a sign you should

29

not ignore, it is a sign for the rest
of you to grow in your confidence and
learn that I call every soul, to abandon its evil conduct of today and turn
to Me wholeheartedly so that she may share
too My Glory;   come, My beloved one,
I, Jesus, love you;

ΙΧΘΥΣ

India   22.1.98

My flower, let this earth exult, may
this whole nation where I have sent
you, marvel at My deeds and be filled

30

with My graciousness ; My blessings are on
these people ... in the presence now of My
angels and saints I tell them : I, Jesus
Christ, Son of God and Saviour am
your help and your shield, turn to Me
and consider all My Commandments ;
learn to be upright and die to yourselves,
My return is imminent ; do not say, " I
have no refuge "; I am your refuge and
My Heart is your resting place ; since
you are so precious in My sight, India,
I have sent to you too My

31

seeds* so that you sow them in your ground and the harvest will be rich and plentiful were you to set your heart to work the soil; and your earth will respond to the grain; then every-one will know of My Love and will respond to My Call; do not shrink back, but come to Me with prayers, I need fervent prayers from your heart for the conversion of the world; in this

* Jesus means the messages of 'True Life in God.'

32

way I will be pleased with you; today, you have heard My Voice* and I tell you: do not waver; do not harden your hearts either, for this is My Grace passing now on you ♡ be one in My Name ♡

ΙΧΘΥΣ ><>

(Later on at 3.45 a.m, Jesus called me.)

tell them : what I need is love, reconciliation and a spirit of forgiveness, yes, I want them to prove their love

* Through the messages of True Life in God.

33

for Me; ic I am with you ....

India 26. 1. 98

I Am; write, My Vassula, My Words for this nation :

I give you My Peace .... let My Peace that I bequeath to you remain with you and envelop you; do not fear and do not say : " what am I to do, Lord ? " India, ah, India, offer Me your heart and pray truthfully from your heart to your Saviour; your prayers will sanctify your soul and those of others; pray

34

without ceasing and make the Evil One flee ..., be united to Me, and be rooted in Me, then no one and nothing in this world will come between you and Me; My great Return is imminent; I have come all the way to you with My Heart in My Hand, take it, India, and place My Heart in your heart; I have come with My Message; I am calling your nation to turn their hearts to God and live holy; I am God and Lord; spread My Love Hymn and make vine-

35

yards everywhere you go; cultivate your land and do not hesitate; do not fear of the tempests that may arise now and then; I Am with you .... My Sacred Heart is your refuge, so come and consecrate yourselves and your families to Me and to the Immaculate Heart of your Mother; I, Jesus, intend to remain in your country and sanctify it; for this, I ask you all to consecrate your country to Our Two Hearts; be loyal to Me and be one in My Name; I bless you,

36

ah, little children ♡ IXΘYΣ 🐟

25. 2. 98

Yahweh, make my love so
intertwined in Yours that You would say:
" welcome to My House ! "

I claim that love is intertwined
with Your Divine Will as well,
and that understanding Your Words
alone, is insufficient, unless we
act on Them too, my Lord;

My Vassula, the shadow of death looming
over your generation, a shadow that can
plunge it into the deepest abyss, is
covering a good part of it now; woe
to those who ensconce so snugly,

37

feeling safe now, these are the ones who play God and say: " Yahweh has no power over us "; confidently sitting on their throne they declare that none can equal them; is there any need to say more? love is missing from within them....

I will speak and you will write; pray that My sayings will clearly ring in the ears of everyone; I have entrusted you with the noblest of My Works in your times; this Divine Work is placed in your hands; yes, it so pleased Me

38

to give It to you and place It with great affection into the hands of a mere child who would have to depend on Me entirely; — * just now I do not want to make it only a passing visit from My Throne to you but give Me your time and I will receive your offer as one who receives garlands of gardenias ....

* Here there was a slight hesitation. I thought God would stop the message, and let me go, but then He said what followed.

39

Ah, my Lord, Your heavenly Presence
is accompanied with the most sublime
fragrances;   So show me, my Lord,
    Your Beautiful Face, and cover
me with Your radiant Light;
    Let me hear Your Voice like a
melody which is ever so sweet, sweeter
    than a thousand honeycombs
    put together.

come then and inhale myrrh coming out
of My Mouth : * — what is the banner
I raised over you?

The banner I see raised over me is **Love**.

yes, love; love is above all; to love is
to do My Will; it is your entry key to

* God paused, then changed the tone of His Voice.

40

My Kingdom in heaven; if you claim you are living in Me and have no love, then you cannot say, you are living in Me; <u>a true life in Me</u>, is to be living the same kind of life as Christ lived; you have heard that it is not those who cry out to Me My Name that shall enter into My Kingdom but only those who, nourished by love,* are doing My Will, while they are still on earth; tell Me, of what use is a fruit-tree which would never produce its fruit?

* Here, love also meant God's Word, & obeying it.

41

or, of what use is a harp without its
strings? in other words, of what use are
to Me your praises when said without
love; of what use are your sacrifices
were they to be offered without love;
your goal then should be love, for it is
on love that in the end you will be
judged and not on your eloquence of
speech or on your knowledge, or on any
of your sacrifices, or on the gifts that
I, in My benevolence offered you, you
will be judged on the measure of your

42

love; these charisms I offered you were so that you build the Church; let your foundation and the structure of your works and of your charisms be built on love so that you do not slacken in doing good; yes, for the good man wins My favour; My City* will be raised on the Blessing of My Holy Spirit .... and the storm will be over .... then, every-creature on earth will be living a

* I knew here that Yahweh meant: " His Reign on earth " by saying the word: " city."

43

true life in Me and their love will be
so intertwined with My Will that their
soul will become the throne of Wisdom;
yes, it is to such as these that Scriptures
say: " the soul of the just is the throne
of Wisdom"; because in the heart
that loved Me there is no lack of
treasure; when My Spirit spoke through
your mouth, My dove, and said: " understanding His Words is insufficient,
unless we act on them"; it was so as to
make you understand that failing to

44

meet in your love with My Divine Will
you will have your Great Fall; so long
as you hang on to this passing world,
you will never understand that it is
in My Holy Spirit that your body could
be captivated, so that your thoughts would
turn into noble thoughts; then in <u>that</u>
divine nobility of thought, and in that
state of divine grace, having absorbed
within you the power of Divinity, in
you will My Work be fulfilled and
My Will be done; and as I have

45

said once before to you all, I say it again: a time will come, and this hour is near, that although you will be still among men, your mind will be in heaven glorifying Our Trinitarian Holiness; and although your body will be moving among men, your soul and mind, captured in My Will, filled with the nobility of My Light, will be as an angel's, and you will find yourself walking in Eden, in Paradise among My angels and saints because your

46

union with Me would be complete ....
ah, and We would be enjoying to see
Ourselves in you; you will have the
image of the unseen God; We will gaze
heaven* in you; you, who would be possessing Us, will be able to lead the kind
of life which We expected of you, a
life which would reach, through perfect
wisdom and spiritual understanding,
the fullest knowledge of My Divine
Will; the life, My dearest children,

* A spiritual heaven

47

you would be leading, you who were created for Our Imperial Courts, would be according to My Mind in all its aspects; I will sanctify you, and you will receive the power to become wholly devout; when all these things*¹ were announced in the Message of Truth*², very few of you understood My Word; today the world hears, but understands nothing, sees, but produces images

*¹ The things that God is telling us now.
*² The Holy Bible

48

that result in nothing; as for those who
seem to be near My Heart and who hold
the keys to My Kingdom, even they have
not understood; yet, they are ardently
longing to offer Me devotions, thanksgiv-
ing, treating their bodies severely,
equaling those whom I crowned with
the crown of glory;* and yet when My
Divine Breath*² blows a scent, a sweet
fragrance upon you, to renew you,
yes, when My Holy Spirit descends

* The Saints
²* The Holy Spirit

49

from the highest heaven putting aflame
the earth as a baptisimal kiss; they
do their best to extinguish the Fire of
My Holy Spirit; today when My Voice
is audible, It frightens them out of their
minds and immediately do everything in
their power to subdue It; I, who am
Author of inestimable marvels, I am
about to open the heavens and let you
know the mystery of My purpose: the
outpouring of My Holy Spirit, Who is
the Promise written in Scriptures, and

50

Who was to act upon My creation like never before in history, lifting them all the way to heaven, approaching everything on earth as near to heaven as it could be possibly done; I, Vassula, who guide all things and decide by My own Will, never broke a promise, but I am known to break down any barrier of division; this is why you should put your hopes in Me, because, as I said, I am about to shatter into smithereens, with the power and the grace of My Holy Spirit, the

51

barriers of your division and unite you,
for My honour, in a single Body; then,
your generation, having come back to their
senses, will cry out to Us:

" adorable Trinity ! hold our
eyes captive on the One Heart and
supply our soul with what it
lacks;

anoint us O Holy and Divine Trinity,
pouring Your oil on us so that we
remain indissolubly united with
You in Your Will and prepare

52

us for Your glorious reign of the
Kingdom on earth in which
Your Will becomes the essence of
our daily life and the emblem on
our forehead, and Love, the
banner above our heads; "
ah, My lily, your Creator tells you this,
so that you go and tell My Own:

"Yahweh, my Lord and most
gracious Father, will adorn us with
His Imperial Vestments, and the earth

53

will be adorned with the hidden
treasures He so kindly kept for our
times; "

I will adorn this earth in Spring, My
Spring; what is the Spring of Yahweh?
My Spring, My beloved ones, will be when
the whole of My creation will be shining with a brilliant light; in the baptism
of the Purification you will be reformed
into your first image; in this Purification
everyone will aspire for a closer union of
love with Me, and in ardour your hearts

54

will search for the Truth, the Way and the Life; and in the Truth, where intoxicating savours will be tasted, your soul, endowed with My Spirit of Grace will be perfected ♡ your image of the dark would be no more, for I, your Bridegroom and the kindest of fathers, will be shining on you;* Love is on the way of return to restore His Kingdom; this will be the reign of My Kingdom on earth and My Will shall be done on earth as it is in heaven;

* *Ap. 22 : 5*

55

so now is the time of repentance; this is
a wicked age but your lives should redeem
it, renounce your will and find favour
with Me by recognizing what is My Will;
ah, Vassula, blessed one of My Call, spread
out My Words in rivers of Mercy and Hope;
be like a lily, in this time of Lent,
unmindful of self, and let your Keeper take
care of you; efface yourself entirely, becoming
like a fluid substance so that you can
flow into Me, your God, becoming one
spirit with Me .... I, God, will

56

meet you any hour of the day you want;
call Me any time, My beloved; so raise
your mind in grateful praise to Me and
extol My Name thrice Holy for having
given you this precious gift : an open gate
to Me ♡

    * the garden of My City,
       state of the State,

    draw with joy from Me: Life;

* Suddenly, Yahweh, my delightful God, spoke in metaphors. With a light shed into my intellect He made
me understand that the 'garden of My City' meant:
'Vassula of My Sanctuary', the same with 'state of
the State.'

57

ah! and be consumed in My Divinity;
do not allow any shadow to cross

your spirit; your Lord graciously
leans towards you now to dress you
with the ornaments of His Love;
I will increase in you, so do not
give in to your weakness, saddening Me
by doubting of My Goodness;
embrace wholeheartedly the precious
dew of divine grace that bornes your
spirit in My Noble Light; you are
invited by Spring Himself ♡

58

My Lord, many great kings
would give their entire Kingdom away
to receive a drop of these graces You
so affectionately offered me in your
immense and divine Love;

I would take the liberty and go on
and say: "Yes! Yes! in a moment
of folly of Your Love, You have
offered me favours in abundance,
dispensing them without measure, and
on what? A mere wretch...."

but you are My chosen one! I saw in
your human frailty, even then,* a glimpse
of what was below the crust of sin,
I saw under these layers of gloom,

* God meant, even before my conversion, that is,
before His divine Call to me.

59

a child-like love, and My Heart upon seeing this was moved to tears; this alone captivated My Mercy; subject to sin, yet a trickle of love was flowing out of you now and then; I then said: "I will set Myself to destroy all that is not Me and revive, by putting aflame, what little is left of Me;" and in the overflowing of My saving grace I acted according to My Will; come now, be like a flaming torch in this darkness of your era; approach Me often so that you

60

taste My sweetness, experiencing delights in this closeness, but revere Me at the same time; A✗Ω

(This message was given to me with several breaks, then at a much later date, the message continued, all the way entering in the month of March, since it was not finished; this was done so because of much travelling for missions.)
March; continuation of previous Message.

My Vassula, I have, together with My Son, Jesus Christ and the Holy Spirit been descending from Our celestial Throne of Glory in Person upon the earth, visiting

61

you in this way to imprint on you Our
Love Theme; We put to you the duty of
passing on Our divine World to many
nations and so you have done what
you were asked to do; you have left
house and family, comfort and land
for the sake of Our Name, My dearest,
and so let Me remind you the reward of
renunciation: for this alone you will
be repaid a hundred times over, and you
inherit My Kingdom which is eternal life;
daughter, on whom I confided this

62

immense treasure, do not listen to antagonistic discussions held in My Name, be like a dove soaring in the air, above all the clamouring and tearing, so do not be distracted and disturbed by exterior things; turn your gaze to Me, remembering that I am yours and that you are Mine; do not be displeased when you are receiving less glorious favours* than in the first three years, because all that is

* Direct answers to my own questions and to those who asked our Lord, through me. Also, constant fragrances, and visions of His Presence.

63

done to you is for My glorification; to
preserve your humility I have done this
act of Wisdom, incomprehensible to you
perhaps, but My act gave you at once the
freedom to come to Me, and work freely
for Me; My act put you in a position
where you would come to Me by your
own free will, lifting your thoughts to
Me, offering Me what you can; and
while I would watch My Own seed giving
her life as an oblation to many, re-
lying on no one but on her Saviour

TRUE LIFE IN GOD

Page 380   Notebook 92

64

who lifted her soul from the valley of death and who drew her into an intimate union in His Heart, I would be rejoicing in My seed; *¹ ... now tell Me, can a man cheat God?

No, never; wearing white *² all the time does not make anyone holier or virtuous, or truthful.

and yet many are cheating the hearts of My children, they are cheating Me

*¹ There was a brief silence.
*² False prophets, and there are <u>many</u> today, many many more than the chosen <u>ones</u> from God. <u>But</u> God is allowing this to happen to test people.

Excerpts from Notebook 93

25 February 98 (continued from Notebook 92)...Tell them what their most gracious Father says: tell them that were they to remain in Me, in My Love, their joy would be complete p. 2.

9 April 98 (Our Lady speaks)...It had been said...there were in the past deceivers, so you too will have your false prophets; p. 7.

✠ My beloved Son is sweetly affected when you and others who have graciously recognized His Merciful Call through His noble theme, sacrifice everything you have for the salvation of souls; p. 10.

✠ Ah! what would He not do in His divine Goodness for all of you! this is something that your philosophers of your times will never grasp; p. 13.

✠ For those who misinterpret Our Divine Messages, be merciful with them, for they know not what they are doing...do not let your tongue condemn them, let the Sole Judge, judge them; p. 14.

19 April 98...Remember, do not get discouraged, look around you, I have gained fruits out of My Divine Work; p. 20.

21 April 98...When your soul does not feel My rays for a while know that at that moment I am refreshing you again; p. 24.

✠ I am preparing you to receive a divine visitation from the Holy Spirit who will entrust you with His Message; p. 25.

22 April 1998...For this noble theme that I will divinely reveal to you, you will have to allow Me to penetrate into your intellect and give you a sublime light of understanding; p. 31.

✠ After My passage through you all... you will see with My Light penetrating even the hidden things of God since you will be seeing things in My radiance; p. 37.

24 April 98...Carry your crosses with love especially the noblest one I passed on to you and the most abhorrent to Satan, the Cross of Unity; p. 41.

✠ My delight, come back to your senses and do not repel My Nails and Thorned Crown that My Love compelled Me to offer you; p. 42.

NB
93

29 May 98...Remember one thing: I, Jesus Christ, the Word of God, will always fulfil all your needs; p. 45.

✠ I want you to keep doing all the things you have learnt from Me and have been taught to do in My Name; do not fear anyone when you assemble together in My Name to Christianize this dechristianized generation; p. 47.

✠ Devote yourself now to My affairs and remember that there is no frontier between you and Me; I am always with you; p. 47.

7 June 98 (Pentecost)...In these days I am descending together with the Father and the Son, as three Witnesses; God the Father is Spirit, (John 4:24) in that He sends Me, the Spirit of Truth, to be with you for ever and lead you to complete Truth; p. 49.

✠ What image, creation, have you contrived of Me and you still do not know Me?...and yet I never stopped testifying; I was never hiding; p. 52.

✠ May your ways remain straight in Our Wisdom so that you may do Our Divine Will; p. 54.

✠ I am trying to draw you all into a filial union of divine Love with the Father and the Son and Myself so that you move in Us and We move in you; p. 55.

✠ With Me your body is alive and in Me and through Me you will be counted as a child of God;...you must allow Me to reign in your hearts and make you sons and daughters of the Most High; p. 56.

✠ Who is born of the Spirit is given a vision of God enabling him to seize Him, acknowledge Him and penetrate in His depths; p. 58.

✠ Be confident and come to Me and from a rebel I will transfigure you into an upright being; p. 59.

✠ Here I am now, becoming knowable to you in this way too, *(by appearing and showing His Face to me)* yet without losing My transcendence; I am filling you with My Knowledge; p. 64.

Notebook 93 — Page 383

by their falsehood;* I tell you, when My Day comes they will be excluded from My Kingdom, on these grounds sentence is pronounced; I have given you by My grace to discern what comes from True Light and what comes from darkness, but I have let you see how many more were drawn to darkness than to Light; I have told you this so that when the time of sorting comes, you

* One of them especially who puts unsparingly God to the test with her false messages, scheming in the dark, deluding many to believe in her; you will know her by her message that declares that "True Life in God" messages stopped in August 1997: a lie that will draw her in her own snare...

2

may remember all that I told you ....*

remember Me to your friends; your
friends are My friends, My dove; tell them
what their most gracious Father says :
tell them that were they to remain in
Me, in My Love, their joy would be complete and everything they would strive for,
for My Sake, in their work, but would
be unable to complete or succeed with
because of their human frailty, I, as a

---

* There was a brief silence, then God spoke of
those who would attend the International Retreat of
TLIG in the Holy Land; they are the organizers
of TLIG & promoters, the sturdy pillars of God's
Message.

3

Father, having seen their nobility of
thought, I would take in consideration
their good intentions for wanting to please
Me; and so I, in My turn, will supply
what would be lacking in them, so
that many would believe in My Work and
Divine Theme of Love; they would believe
not because of them but in the evidence
of the perfect Work that will be accomplished in My Divinity; —* and you,

* The Lord's gaze turned towards me; His look was
friendly and fatherly at the same time.

4

My dove, behold the Bridegroom who lifted you and directed you by His Spirit in His calling; * sing a psalm to Me by saying :

> Fountain of Living Water,
> preserve my soul in times of trouble,
> keep my soul cleaved on Your Heart,
> where the Springs of Yahweh refresh
> and exult every heart that comes

* While the Lord of Goodness was saying these words, my soul was lifted to the heights, to glimpse His Glory, giving me a slight taste of the vision of Beatitude.

5

to rest in this inmost Center of Love;

O behold the One who clothed Me
with His Imperial Vestments* in order
to draw unsparingly nation after nation
to muster round the whole Blessed
Trinity in one body ♡

behold His ♡ infinite Graciousness, Who delights even in my miser-
able heart, as though there were
no other creatures save myself;

blessed be Yahweh for ever; amen;

* Meaning Christ Himself

6

yes! I have given you Life in My Divinity, smouldering your imperfections; and now, joined and inseparably united to Divinity Himself, I bless you thrice in My Name; may your achievements bring prosperity to all mankind; do them in keeping My Name Holy, and live at peace with everyone;

A ☧ Ω

7

9. 4. 98

Our Lady speaks:

My Vassula, My Presence is Peace and Joy, yes, for I am your Mother before your mother on earth; I share, as a mother shares with her children, your joys, your sufferings and all you endure; it is giving Me great joy to see My children living the life of truth as they were commanded from the beginning by the Eternal Father; today My Vassula, there are many deceivers, but it had been said that as there were in the past

TRUE LIFE IN GOD

8

deceivers¹*, so you too will have your false prophets; in the beginning they would try to buy you for themselves²*, then very quickly would turn against you once they realize their malice is uncovered in the light of the Truth by the Spirit to you; ah, My child, I have you wrapped up in My Immaculate Heart, this is the way I protect My children; in My unfailing Love I have for all of you, I, as a

¹
* Our Lady means false prophets
²
* By a flow of flattering messages personally to you.

9

Mother, will always be your gracious Protector and Defender; why, have you not heard how I become like a lioness who defends her cubs when defiled hands stretch out to touch you? no one will be able to take you away from Me; you are, My Vassula, consecrated to Me, and you have signed your consecration to Me with your own blood*, and with this, God confirmed you, strengthened and

---

* I had pricked my finger and signed then with my own blood the consecration to become the Slave of our Blessed Mother.

10

supported you, for His grace and His
power lasts for ever and ever; My Son,
Jesus Christ is always near you and has
your hand clasped into His so that you
will never be separated from Him;
My beloved Son is sweetly affected when
you and others who have graciously recognized His Merciful Call through His
noble theme, sacrifice everything you have
for the salvation of souls;   and God,
the Father, who is the kindest of fathers,
who favoured you amongst thousands,

II

giving you this inestimable gift and teaching you with Wisdom, filling your mind
and those of others with everything
that is true, everything that is noble,
everything that is good and pure; in His
irresistible Love He has for all His creatures,
the Creator has blessed you thrice from
His Throne; in His royal courts He raised
you* with nectar from His Mouth, and

* All of a sudden, while hearing these words, I understood an old vision I had, when I was taken in the
spirit in our Father's House with many rooms,
and with a Banquet laid out for us. In
the vision I was led to go to a room, with

12

a veranda. What was striking in my vision was the great peace all around. After going out of that room, I had then heard babblings of a child from the nearby room, for the door was somewhat open. I did not have to go inside the room to see, but I saw, in the vision, with the eyes of my soul, who was inside that other room. I saw a lady sitting on a wooden bench, looking at the child that babbled and who was sitting on the floor, by this lady's feet.

— At the time of the vision, I never understood who these two were, since God did not reveal to me their identity.

But now, with the words of our Blessed Mother, this mystery was revealed to me. The lady was our Blessed Mother and the child was me. I was looking at my-self. I was in the courts of my Father who truly raised me with nectar, and my Mother was watching over me, while all one could hear in that awsome silence was a child's babblings. (Vision of 22.11.86)

13

from His Majestic Throne, God reached you
to console you and through you,
millions of others who were in desperate need
of consolation; ah! what would He not
do in His divine Goodness for all of
you! this is something that your philosophers
of your times will never grasp because it
is something that does not fit into their
way of thinking; rejoice exceedingly, daughter,
for you have received graces more than you
could ever merit; praise the Holy Spirit
of God too, who descended softly and

14

gently from above upon you, to befriend you; anoint you and instruct you the Way; so glorify the Forerunner who flooded you with His Love and made you taste His intimate sweetness, lifting you on His Wings to soar the skies with Him; so be not afraid .... so long as you are grafted on My Immaculate Heart, be not afraid ... pray, My Vassula, for those who misinterpret Our Divine Messages, be merciful with them, for they know not what they are doing .... take pity on their

15

desolation and do not let your tongue condemn them, let the Sole Judge, judge them; will you do this for Me?

I will try, I will try to remember.

try .... be eternally good, My Vassula, and be patient ♡ do not let temptations of this kind assail you and disfigure your soul; let the One who is the Highest delight in you; expiate for them instead, and every time you will expiate, the Good Lord will anoint you with the unction of His Divine Love for your gesture, and His

16

Face will shine on you and He will ex-
ecute His Blessings on mankind; act as
God wants you to act; release Me from
the pains My Heart succumbs to daily
from those who deny the real Presence of
My Son in the Eucharist; Jesus affectionately invites you to partake of His Body; know
that He desires you with all His Heart
and, any generous gesture from your part,
His Heart melts into Rivers of Mercy and
Goodness which flow on many hardened
hearts .....

17

*

O Royal Virgin,
inseparably united to Jesus' Heart,
I offer You all the sinners of the
world who offend Your Son in the
Blessed Sacrament,
may they who strike Him, be
forgiven by God through Your
Innocence, Your Blessedness and
Your Sweet Heart which became
the Holiest Tabernacle of God;
amen;

amen; trust God, My Vassula, because He
has the power and the Wisdom to approach
the guilty and straighten their path ....
be disposed for the Lord to give Him
praise and glory; He will reveal*² to you

*¹ My soul suddenly filled with the Spirit, cried out.
* The subjects of teachings I had to prepare for
the TLIG international meeting.

18

His intentions; remain in God's Peace;
I bless you;

19. 4. 98

Lord ?

I Am; peace be with you; let it be known:
the mouths that shout calumny to you,
are shouting calumny to My gifts on you;
they will have that sin lying heavily
on themselves unless they come foreward
and repent ! I will repeat what I have
already said to you, I have joined your
heart to Mine forever and My promises

19

stand firm; I have joined your heart to Mine in such a way to secure it, that there is no way of uprooting it; you are, My dove, well-rooted in what gives life and freedom; My precious child, calm your heart and do not pay attention to the violence of calumnies said on you, little do they know that they are calumniating Me and not you, giving Me impressive wounds on My Body; those who persist with violence to calumniate My Work in their deficiencies, will

20

have in the end their share ....

in My Infinite Love, I will increase in you and while My Head will be resting on your heart, I will continue to murmur in your ear My Love and My words of salvation and deliverance;

pupil remember, do not get discouraged; look around you; I have gained fruits out of My Divine Work, so lift your face to Me and smile, smile and make Me happy;

21

I have now understood that in our close
union, our Good Lord feels everything.
Even if we feel unhappy, He becomes
unhappy because we are unhappy;

now allow Me to repose in My heaven*
while you reflect on My Words ♡

ΙΧΘΥΣ ⊂◦==▷

21. 4. 98

May the sweetness of the Lord
    be on us!' (Ps 90: 17)

ah, enter into the joy of your Lord!
yes? say it!   (I had a complaint)

* Our Lord means : 'let Me repose in your heart.'

22

Why do You private me of Your companionship?

come, say what you want to say ....

and You do it as though You take Your pleasure in it by bringing forth all sorts of events that obstruct me from using the gift You have given me and being thus in Your delightful Presence which is Light.

I have given you a wreath that will never wither, and I have baptised you with Fire; I have given you spiritual food and drink; how is it that at moments you fail to understand Me? I would have given you now a sharp

23

answer, but considering your words pronounced to Me the other day,* coming out
from the depths of your heart, know
that I am reluctant in mortifying you;
I am still perfumed by your words of
love, I have received your words as a
sweet fragrance of myrrh and My hair
is covered with drops of your aromatic
words and My head is all perfumed,

* While I was preparing some speeches that I would
read out in the presence of the responsible people
of True Life in God, I was seized by the Spirit of
God and wrote:" Today God the Father invites us in the nuptial chamber of His Heart;

24

this is the final goal that everyone should
attain in their spiritual life! — God invites
us all to plunge in His Bosom and
lose ourselves within Him. (Here are
those words that touched our Lord):
"I, personally, would like to become
like liquid in God or sometimes go
as far as to dissolve so completely
into God that I would be no more."

you have bound* Me with your words ....
but I tell you, this act of privation
is so that I ripen your fruits; yes, I
am your Sunshine, but a tree needs
rain as well to be able to grow and
multiply its foliage and its fruit; when

* This word should be taken in the good sense.

25

your soul does not feel My rays for a while, know that at that moment I am refreshing you again; and now tell Me, how does your soul feel right now?

right now I feel enamoured by Divine Grace ....

cease then tormenting your soul and reproaching Me; be grateful instead for all the graces I have poured in your soul; I am preparing you to receive a divine visitation from the Holy Spirit who will entrust you with His Message * and who

* Look at page 30, date 22.4. 98

26

would leave with His Noble Theme an everlasting memory to this generation and to
all future generations; My tender spouse,
be of Jesus as Jesus is of you; I am
for you as you are for Me[*]; we are one
for the other and so complete in union
and intertwined that a number of
souls have seen Me in you and you in Me[*2];

[*] Here Jesus means in the sense of belonging.

[*2] In the Madrid incident. Many people in different
nations have seen our Lord's Face appear on my
face, but for the 2nd time Jesus allowed His Face
to look like mine. In Madrid a man looked
at the big poster of Jesus' Face and was

27

asking the organizers of my meeting why
were they putting up a poster of a blond
woman.

The first time this happened it was in
Greece, Rhodos. The prayer group of True
Life in God were going to a hospital for
charity to evangelize and console the sick,
always accompanied by the priest of the
hospital.   One day they decided to distri-
bute Jesus' portrait printed on a small post-
card, a famous image of Jesus which is on
the island of Patmos in the monastry, known
to have shed tears.   The priest came to them
quite upset, and had collected back all the
pictures; furiously he asked: 'why are you
distributing Vassula's picture?' Surprised, the
girls asked him which picture, and he
showed them Jesus' portrait. They told
him that it was Jesus, showing him His
beard. The priest remained silent....

let Me delight and contemplate Myself

28

in you; I enjoy immensly those moments
when I gaze at Myself; I have indeed
clothed you with Myself to possess you
and have offered you My Grace to possess
Me in Grace; call it if you wish: the
folly of God, enamoured of his creation
to folly *; see? therefore, calm down
your heart and understand those moments
of privation ♡

* At this moment, our Lord was reminding
me of another word which is often mentioned
in Scriptures: ' the jealous love of God.'

29

I know that had You not shown Yourself to me in the beginning (1985) I would be still out there in the graveyard among the putrefied; had it not been for Your Grace, I would have by now putrefied myself;

My soul was longing for You when You were prolonging Your rains upon me ....

but now, My dove, have I not released you from your pains? hear Me, Vassiliki: know that while you were in the state of privation I was resting in your heart .... be blessed and find your comfort in My Heart; ΙΧΘΥΣ

30

22. 4. 98

This divine message that was foretold by Jesus on the 21st April 1998, has been given to me by the the third Divine Person of the Holy Trinity: the Holy Spirit. I was called by His Divine grace every now and then to write it. It ended up on the 29 of July 1998. — The Holy Spirit speaks:

peace be with you; the theme that I am about to reveal to you for the glory and the benefit of the Church, this Church which Christ bought with His Own Blood, is going to be one of the noblest themes about Myself; it is necessary that I manifest these riches to

31

your brothers and sisters so that they
too nourish themselves on these inexhaus-
tible riches that flow down in abundance
to benefit the Church; divert your thoughts
and turn your attention fully to Me
now*; for this noble theme that I
will divinely reveal to you, you will
have to allow Me to penetrate into
your intellect and give you a sublime
light of understanding; I will stoop
in My benevolence to speak not only to
you, but Prodigy Himself will dispose

* This was said for me..

32

His Knowledge to all mankind; behold,
the Bridegroom is stooping over you to
communicate to you all words of Life
that will adorn you all with royal
purple; by grace, you will receive from Me,
if you open your heart, sanctifying graces
which will invigorate your soul and lead
you into perfection; those who would read
these words of Life and are undisposed
and not in the truth, will see everything as nonsense, for accustomed to
walk with Sterility, they will not be

33

touched; but for those who seek Paradise
in simplicity of heart and who do not put
Me to the test, on those will I shed My
Light and Rays and I will illuminate
them; I will then make My way in them
and purify them; and when they will
come trembling to the reckoning of their
impurity and sins, with a groan that
will sound more of a new-born's wailing,
they will give birth to a new life in Me,
capitulated by Jealous Love; after having
conquered them in Blessedness, I shall

34

flow like a vivifying River inside them.
My vivifying passage within them will
not go by unnoticed; I will not be like
a ship that cuts through heaving waves
and leaves no trace to show where it passed, or like a bird flying through the
air, leaving no proof of its passing or
a sign of its passage. I will
come to them and wed them and
clothe them with Christ; I will transfigure their soul into an Eden because
they would be carrying God within them

35

as their lamp; this will be the sign given to
them in My invincible Holiness, I will remain in
them taking care of them; and I Myself
will be the One who will adorn them with
bridal vestments; crowning them with My
Deity, a royal crown of splendour, the
diadem beauty from the Hand of the
Trinity; no one is worthy of such favours,
but in My ineffable Love, I said: "night
now must yield to light, vice to virtue;"
I will work in their soul so that
temperance, prudence, justice and fortitude

36

will be their wealth; ah, Vassula, I will cultivate your generation and make them understand that immortality is found in being kin to Us the Triune God; what is more wealthy than this Work of Mercy I, God, will be doing in them? then, having breathed Life in these souls, I will despatch Wisdom from My throne of glory to become their Prodigy; — then everything that had been reduced to ashes in the sterility of this earth through all these years, I, in My divine benevolence, will

37

make anyone who is willing, revive and
blossom; fecundated by My warm rays of
light, I tell you, generation, you will be
divinized and deified in Our Trinitarian
Deity; today, My Vassula, everyone sees as
far as they are able to see, but after My
passage through you all, you will not be
limited and see the way you see now,
but, in a most ineffable manner and
most divine, you will see with My Light
penetrating even the hidden things of God
since you will be seeing things in My

38

radiance* ; your entire body will be shining with a brilliant light ; I will be the lamp of your body²* that will fill it with the splendours of Our Kingdom, which are: soundness, gentleness, love, mercy, joy, peace, patience, truthfulness, goodness and kindness ; from the beginning We made you in the image of Our Own Nature ; We had said: " let Us make mankind in Our Own Image, yes, in the likeness of Ourselves ; " but it

¹* The Holy Spirit is foretelling us of the 'era of the Spirit'
²* Mt 6: 22 + 23

39

was the devil's envy that brought you all to death; now the earth groans with pain, chastising itself, sighing and crying, weary of no longer being, tearful and suffocating for lack of air*, moulding in its interiour and putrefying in its entrails; yes, you have ceased to be .... come, My Vassula, this will do for now; be one with Me! (Here the Holy Spirit stopped His divine dictation to me and He made me understand that He will continue His Message later on; see p. 48)

* I understood this as: Lack of the Holy Spirit blowing on us because of the earth's prohibition of the Holy Spirit to act freely on us. In truth we can say that the Holy Spirit is stifled beyond imagination by this generation.

40

24. 4. 98

" When a man's rights are overridden
in defiance of the Most High, when a man
is deprived of justice, does not the
Lord see it? "　　Lm 3: 35 - 36

Vassula, adversity practised on you
gladens Me !*¹

And I, only yesterday, on Saint
George's feast day, I was pleading
him to intercede for me and take
away my adversaries!

ah, no, no, no, no!* why should I let
you by your own foolishness lose the
crown of the faithful I have

* Jesus was extremely cheerful; He was
　really full of joy; somehow He
surprised me.
²
* These "no-s" were said quickly as though one word.

41

prepared for you, and everything else I
have stored up for you in heaven!

this is the sort of love I showed to all
of My chosen ones; so will you stop your
unfounded thoughts?... come, foolish little
child, remain united to Me who am the
Head* and you will receive the strength you
need to bear anything joyfully; I will
never neglect you; carry your crosses
with love, especially the noblest one I passed
on to you and the most abhorrent to
Satan, the Cross of Unity, and do not

* The Head of the Church.

42

be afraid to suffer adversity; it is after all for My glory!

> O Lord, You know I've prayed to Saint George, so now what will become of my request to him?

Saint George, who died as a martyr, will protect you from all evils; he is by your side and guards you; he will pray so that your thoughts would be focused on heavenly things; so then, My delight, come back to your senses and do not repel My Nails and Thorned Crown that My

43

Love compelled Me to offer you; rose of the Rose*[1] I have crowned you with My Jewels*[2]; I am lenient to many things but to dispose of these Jewels? never! come! come to Me and taste the flow of sweetness coming out of My Mouth, this sweetness will reassure you that from all Eternity you were Mine and I was yours .... I am now on My way, dearest one, but only for a little while to allow you to continue your good

---

* I understood this as meaning: heart of the Heart.
* Our Lord means with His Redemptive Instruments

44

work;[*]   ΙΧΘΥΣ

29. 5. 98

In the unrelenting pain of my spirit I must
speak, lament in the bitterness of my
   soul; come, I beg You, look at
   me; have You done away with me?
my roots are thrust in You, yet in
my silence I say: " The Lord God surely
is upset with me; He will surely cut me
   off one of these days; " I look for
light to understand, but there is only
darkness; have I been maybe insensitive
   to Your Goodness? have I disappointed
You in any way or neglected You? or
   has the sight of the sun in its glory,
or the glow of the moon as it walked
   the sky, stolen my heart from You,
so that my hand blew them a kiss?

* Jesus means my housework.

45

My loving spouse, allow Me to pour on you My sweet fragrance, and remember one thing: I, Jesus Christ, the Word of God, will always fulfil all your needs*; numerous are your failures, but I had foreseen all of this, before even I announced My Message to you ♡ but I have given you, in My immeasurable Love I have for you, a place in Me, where in that particular place I could bring your soul in the perfection I demand of My saints; ah, Vassula, overflowing clemency

* Jesus means my negligences and failures

46

is Me, fathomless love is Me, and yet, you <u>still</u> know Me so little, My dove; why these obscure thoughts of Me? everything I have <u>is</u> yours and forever*; be then of good cheer and spare Me from this unnecessary Cup; the Word of Life was given to you freely so that you, in your turn, give it freely to the others; I had a pattern in My Work, as you see,

* Our Lord was saying these words very slowly with a <u>sad</u> Voice for being still misunderstood by the creature He has given, in His divine benevolence, so much.

47

and I want you to keep doing all the
things you have learnt from Me and
have been taught to do in My Name;
do not fear anyone when you assemble
together in My Name to christianize this
dechristianized generation; everything you do
is for My honour and My glory. I am
building; it is I who do the building, and woe to those who stretch
their hand to destroy what is being
constructed by Me! devote yourself
now to My affairs and remember that

48

there is no frontier between you and Me;
I am always with you, My beloved;
I bless you; ic

Sunday, Pentecost*   7. 6. 98

(The Holy Spirit continues His Divine Message
of the 22. 4. 98.)

ah .... My Vassula .... I have chosen you and
I have not rejected you although you too
had ceased to be; and so it will be that
I will show in this same manner My ineffable
affection and My divine power to anyone who

* The Orthodox Calendar

49

is willing; * I will not reject you but see how lenient My Love for you compels Me to be? in these days I am descending together with the Father and the Son as three Witnesses; God the Father is Spirit, in that He sends Me, the Spirit of Truth, to be with you for ever and lead you to the com-

* The Holy Spirit speaks to the whole world now.

* Jn 4:24 . St Paul too in 1 Cor 15:45 speaks of Christ as " life-giving Spirit ".
The description " Spirit " in the biblical sense does not define God's nature so much as it describes His life-giving activity.
God is Spirit in that He gives the Spirit.

* Jn 14:17

50

plete Truth; the Word of God, Light and
Saviour and who existed since the beginning,
who is nearest to the Father's Heart, has
witnessed and made the Father known to
you; you have been bought and paid for
with His own Blood; have you not read
that the Word of God is alive and active
and testifies on earth as I and the Father
testify? the Holy One who bought His
Church with His own Blood* testifies with
His Blood and I, the Holy Spirit of
Truth, who leads you to the complete

* With this Sacrifice we obtained Eternal Life

51

Truth* testify with Water*; therefore, We
are three Witnesses and all three of Us
agree as We are One, God alone*, with one

---

* In John 16 : 12-13 Jesus says to His disciples: " I still
have many things to say to you but they would be
too much for you now; but when the Spirit of Truth
comes He will lead you to the complete Truth ... "
   It is a mistake to speak of an end to Revelation
and treat it as a deposit of sentences . God is active
and alive and will continue showing Himself through
the Holy Spirit, never stopping in doing so.
    When one says in Latin : " completere",
it means that Christ is the full, complete revelation of God; and not that He will stop
revealing Himself to mankind. — The Holy
Bible is the narrative testimony of Jesus
Christ. It is not God's last word.

*2   With Baptism   *3 In the unity of essence

52

Will, one Power and one Dominion; what image, creation, have you contrived of Me and you still do not know Me? .... and yet I never stopped testifying; I was never hiding ....*

* At this moment, I saw a Face inundated with light, fairer than the fairest angel. The Unformed took form; in this vision of the Holy Spirit, who wanted to show Himself out of His boundless love, an undeserved gift to an unworthy being as myself, left my heart rejoicing; every time the memory of this vision returned to me, my heart anew rejoiced. It cannot fade away from my memory; this vision of His Holy Face is going to remain with me for ever.

53

" O Ineffable Light of Beauty, Your Divine
Eyes, were soft and smiling; You smiled
at me and I found myself smiling back
at You; Your Face O Holy One contained
an angelic charm; Your Holy Face radia-
ting Love and Purity was ever so near
mine; I was not even in profound medi-
tation when You surprised me by appearing to
me; " although His Face was altogether
adorable, His Eyes were the ones which drew
my attention, leaving me in awe and in ad-
miration; " the love of Your gaze looking
into mine with ineffable tenderness were like
two glittering stars, they were like a turquoise
transparent sea filled with serenity; what
can I, the poor worm say?
      Your Divine Eyes my Lord
are like a Liturgy, an ocean of Love,
a Paradise and a consuming fire for
   the one who undeservedly was
allowed to contemplate them...., "

54

how blessed you are, you whose ears I opened, may your ways remain straight in Our Wisdom so that you may do Our Divine Will; count on Me, beloved, for I will bring as many as possible in union with Our Oneness and I will fill them with Light so that they will be filled with the absolute fullness of Our Trinitarian Deity; — come and learn:

in hardships I am always with you; I am your Consoler and where there is despair I console and heal; I am the Giver of

55

Life and with My baptisimal kiss I blow on you, I renew you; I renew you so that your natural inclinations that are so opposed to God and ever so human and worldly, leading you to death, can be transformed and deified in My Divinity and My Nobility and become as those of the angels and saints; I am trying to draw you all into a filial union of divine Love with the Father and the Son and Myself, so that you move in Us and We move in you; I can transform your imprisoned minds

56

and free them so that your thoughts and
sayings will be only on spiritual things;
therefore do not say: "I am doomed by
Satan's baptismal kiss of death;" no!
not if you come to Me now; I am the
antidote to Satan's deathly kiss; I am
the antidote to Death itself .... it is true
that without Me your body is dead, but
with Me your body is alive and in Me
and through Me you will be counted as
a child of God; this is why you
must allow Me to reign in your hearts

57

and make you into sons and daughters
of the Most High ; Scripture says* : "happy
the pure in heart : they shall see
God!" in order to see God, and acknowledge Him as your Father you have to
be born of Me, the Holy Spirit, by
grace; how else would you see God?
a child, before being born, has he
ever seen his father? not until he is
born will he see his father; and so it
is with your spiritual birth of Me; flesh

* Mt 5:8

58

is flesh and has the vision of flesh; but who is born of the Spirit is given a vision of God enabling him to seize Him, acknowledge Him and penetrate in His depths; so come and advance your step, go forward, and I will carry you on My Wings to soar the skies and bring you in Our adoption place, there where all My saints are, anointed by Us thrice Holy; why, did you not know that you too have an assigned place among them? be confident and come

59

to Me and from a rebel I will transfigure you into an upright being, leading
your soul into sanctification and then
sin will no longer have any power
over you; sin is like an evil master in
you and you should not give that master
any opportunity in any instance to over-
rule you; but I, who am the Source of
all that is Good can overpower your
evil master which is sin, because My Law
is a Law of Goodness and Life, overpower-
ing all your evil inclinations; come and

60

find Me in simplicity of heart and fasten your heart on Me; do not come to Me with mistrust nor with brilliance of worldly speech; do not approach Me with conceit, vice or deceitfulness, no one who comes in that manner ever seizes Me or sees Me, but the souls who walk in the light of contrition and innocence will not be deprived from My Presence; I will fly to them from My Glory in a brilliant light, followed by myriads of angels to heal them, renewing them

61

and making them one spirit with Mine
to inherit My Kingdom; flesh and blood
cannot inherit My Kingdom, for what is
perishable cannot inherit what lasts for
ever; then to make you understand
who is the Unique, Trinitarian God,
yet One in the unity of essence, I will
be healing your guilt, flowing in you
as a river, refreshing your aridity and
sterility; no one is worthy to see God,
indeed, were anyone perfect among you,
if he lacked the Wisdom and the Light

62

that comes from Me, he would still
count for nothing; the depths of God
are riches which are not of this world,
and to contain them without Me is
impossible; to penetrate God's motives
or understand His methods without Me,
is impossible, but were you to allow Me
to be recognized in your consciousness, penetrating your intelligence, I will model you
in Myself to be truly pleasing to Us;
your abandonment to Me is the only
way I could transform your mind

63

to have the mind of Christ, discovering
Our Will and knowing what is good
and what it is that We want and
what is the perfect thing to do; so do
not allow your flesh* to protest .... although
I seem to appear inaccessible to the eye
and unattainable, unseen altogether, I
let Myself be seen in full clarity; I utter
words of Wisdom and as a friend who
confides himself to a friend I confide
My secrets to you, hiding none of them

* Here it means human spirit,

64

from you; I face you, and I, the formless
one, take form in your spirit;[*1]   ah,
Vassula, I am altogether a reflection of
the eternal light and as an untarnished
mirror My Magnificence is magnified in all
the creation; here I am now, becoming
knowable to you in this way too[*2]; yet
without losing My transcendence; I am
filling you with My Knowledge, even though
this flow of transcendent light which I

_____

[*1] At this moment, again the same vision appeared
to me, the vision of the Holy Spirit's Face
inundated in an ineffable light.

[*2] By appearing and showing His Face to me.

Excerpts from Notebook 94

21 June 1998...I have revealed to you and to others Christ's mind, even as Christ revealed to you the mind of the Father; p. 3.

⊕ I am your Helper but so is the Father and Christ; you have now contemplated the One who encompasses all beings; p. 4.

⊕ I am the inner Source of Christian Unity, and it is in Me you should put your hopes and your union;...I am the vivifying Spirit of the risen Son and the vivifying breath of your mortal bodies; p. 5.

⊕ Together with the Father and the Son, I tell you: love the Unique Trinitarian God with all your heart, with all your soul and with all your mind; p. 9.

22 June 1998...I am the inner Source of power within you whose sweetest melodies sung to you resound in every nation; p. 10.

⊕ Were I to find your spirit eager and thirsty to know Me...I would fly to you at your first invitation and sign you with My fiery baptismal kiss on your forehead; p. 12.

⊕ I will revive your love for the gospel to equal your eagerness to that of the first apostles and to spread the gospel of peace; p. 13.

⊕ I will privilege you to grow in your love not only for Us, but also for your brothers and sisters; p. 14.

⊕ In Me, you will enjoy freedom; without Me your soul remains captive and will fall in the snares of the evil one who will imprison you; p. 16.

⊕ Encourage your generation to get to know the Father; tell them that He is a gentle Father and a God of consolation; p. 19.

⊕ For their salvation I raised prophets to help them understand and reach the fullest knowledge of Our Divine Will; p. 24.

⊕ All the saints and angels declare now with one melodious voice: "We thank you O most Holy and adorable Trinity, Eternal Wisdom, for supplying, in an ineffable abyss of generosity, the whole world with Your Canticle of Hope and Love;" p. 25.

NB
94

✠ Your spring flowers, since they would blossom in Spring Himself, will perfume the earth, and the earth, revived by your
aromatic fragrance, will utter its first word: "Father!" and
it will be saved; p. 33.

✠ You have been favoured by the odor of My fragrance *(His
Holy Presence)* and I allowed you to contemplate My Holy
Face which shone on you; p. 36.

✠ You have been taught that the lamp of your body is your
eye...I am this lamp and anyone who has Me within him
will seek the true virtues and not vices; p. 38.

✠ I refreshed you and nourished you to grow in virtue; I gave
you such virtues as love and patience, wisdom, knowledge, fortitude and perseverance; p. 41.

✠ In the beginning, Christ instructed you as well as the Father,
through Me, that we would be sending you...where iniquity and vice is worn like a crown on those who recrucify
Christ; p. 45.

✠ Although from the exteriour you appeared frail, I rendered
you strong from within, proof that I am well within you
and that your virtue is indeed rooted in the Truth; p. 46.

✠ **Canticle of the Bridegroom**...I deify all those to whom I am
united and they no longer speak with their own mind but
in the manner I would speak...their acts would be My acts;
p. 56.

✠ *(Vassula:)* Jesus leaned His beautiful Head and graciously
kissed the interior of my right hand, then placed it on His
Cheek, manifesting his tenderness and love; p. 63.

✠ *(Jesus:)* Winnow good from evil; ecclesia will revive, My beloved one; I bless you; I am with you; p. 64.

am pouring in you goes beyond what you can contain*; I offer, nevertheless, all those treasures of Our Kingdom to adorn not only your soul, but all of the others too; I am, for those who love Me, indeed more resplendent than the sun, outshining all the constellations put together, and as I transcend, I can fill all things with My brightness without being contained by their limits; this is the way I deploy My light in your soul, ordering all things within you to be good so that you, in

* In other words, beyond my capacity.

2

your turn reflect My Goodness and grow
in virtue;

(continuation)   21. 6. 98

Ah, my Joy right now is great,
You fill my soul not only with
Your transcendent light but with joy too.

yes, My beloved, My wealth is Joy as well;

You are my Comforter in times of
anxiety, in times of sorrow; You console
my soul, O perfect One; may You
assist my soul in Your loving Tenderness

O Glorious Throne, my God,
Set high from all Eternity, come
and uproot all evil from within
Your sanctuary and show me
Compassion, show me Your Holy
Countenance ....

3

My sympathy is with you, My weak child;
I have revealed to you and to others Christ's
mind, even as Christ revealed to you the
mind of the Father; do not doubt of My
power; do not doubt of My favour I
conferred on you to be able to hear Me,
understand Me and this time gaze at Me;
I have emptied you by grace and filled
you with Myself; so be happy, I want
you always happy, for heaven is your
homeland; I have, Vassula, through
all these years, satisfied you with the

4

melody of My Voice, first in your heart
and in your mind, then I granted
you now one more unmerited favour:
to gaze at Me in this one manifestation;
I am your Helper but so is the Father
and Christ; you have now contemplated
the One who encompasses all beings;
you must not be surprised when the
world today remains dead to My Call,
and when it listens but does not
understand; so long as they are ruled over
by the evil one, clinging to this passing

5

world, I will remain for them unknown;
I am the inner Source of Christian Unity,
and it is in Me you should put your
hopes and your union; I am the Source
of Hope, Faith and Love; Infinitely rich, I
glory in My glory; I am the vivifying
Spirit of the risen Son and the
vivifying breath of your mortal bodies;
and so you who live for Us, you will
be vitalized by My Divine Power to be
destined for glory; not only do I re-
surrect you, but I also give you a free

6

way to enter Our glory, becoming Our adoptive child and heir to Our Kingdom; I have said to you that I am the Source of Hope because, were you to accept Me as your Helper, you would be accepting Hope and I who know how to express your plea, I would be expressing it with words of Wisdom and according to Our Mind, in a way that would be pleasing to Us; I am your Hope, since I made My home in you; so be content to hope that you shall be saved and risen by

7

Me; enjoy the freedom I am giving you
and possess Me as I would be possessing
you, then, only then would My Reign
begin in you .... it begins when your
soul will become as beautiful as a bride
dressed for her husband in her nuptial
gown; you will then realize with tears
in your eyes that you were not made
to remain celibate but that you were
My promised one and that I, the Holy
Spirit, your promised One, the Bridegroom
of all creation would sanctify your

8

soul in My embraces and in royal munificence; did you forget, My beloved,
how, not long ago before our wedding,
your soul at night was longing for Me
and how your spirit too was seeking Me?
see now how delicious My Love is? see
how Our Triune Holiness and Tenderness
expand like sweet fragrance all around
the universe, perfuming it? all souls to
which I am joined become brides, for in
Our intimacy We draw them in Us
to become their Bridegroom each day

9

of their life ; and they, enamoured of Us,
willingly thrust themselves in Us and ever
so completely to savour the fullness of Our
Divine Love that they become one with
Us .... now, My dearest soul, have your
rest in Me and remain My triumph*;
together with the Father and the Son,
I tell you: love the Unique Trinitarian
God with all your heart, with all your
soul and with all your mind; We bless
you for dedicating your time to Us and

* Because the Holy Spirit conquered me.

10

for serving Us ;

(continuation)   22. 6. 98

come daughter .... I am the inner Source
of power within you whose sweetest melodies
sung to you resound in every nation; have
I not written for you, My dove,
thousands of pages of love, counsel and
knowledge, for you to be able to expound
the Truth in this impoverished generation?
have I not, My bride, filled you with
sound words to answer those who question
you? it is from Me that you breathe,

11

bathed in My Light; it is in Me that
you move and are* never ceasing to be; for
My Majesty transcends earth and heaven
and all that is within them; then,
from My Mouth, full of grace, flow wealth
and honour, enriching all those who love
Me; enriching them to know Us as
Triune, yet One in the unity of essence;
teaching them with tenderness of heavenly
realities, lifting their spirit to revolve
only around heavenly realities; it was I

* It can be taken as: exist

12

who created your inmost self and put
you together in your mother's womb; —
and as I watched daily, inebriated with
delight, your bones taking shape, forming
in secret, I was already celebrating our
betrothals; I tell you, were I to find
your spirit eager and thirsty to know
Me, I, who, from your birth was so
eager to possess you and espouse you
to Myself, I would fly to you at your
first invitation and brand you with
My fiery baptismal kiss on your

13

forehead; a heavenly sign of our matrimonial celebration; then, My loved one,
I would crown you with a wreath of
the most fragrant flowers; each of its
petals representing a virtue; I am the
Gateway through which the virtuous
enter. and as My word has guaranteed,
I will revive your love for the gospel
to equal your eagerness to that of the
first apostles to spread the gospel of
peace; and everywhere you would go,
you would leave behind you My scent,

14

perfuming nation after nation, for I would always be with you; I will privilege you to grow in your love not only for Us, but also for your brothers and sisters, so that you sing to Us the psalm:* " how good, how delightful it is for all to live together like brothers ... " I will become your personal Helper and Companion and also your family, your brother, your sister;

Ps 133 : 1

15

I will become your bearer*[1]; I will become your amen to 'the Amen'*[2] and your canticle to the One who hymns to you now ....

I will reveal to you, My bride, what flesh and blood can never reveal to you: I will reveal to you the innermost part of your heart and the depths and the mind of God too; I will show My favour graciously by increasing in you while I will be decreasing you; Dawn

---

* The Carrier and Dispenser of a variety of Gifts.

* Meaning: your amen to Faithful and True; a name given to God.

16

will be waking in you while Night will be dying in you; I am the Light of your soul and beautiful as a Parousia in you I will shine and inaugurate with all My angels and saints Our union of divine Love; We shall celebrate our espousals .... in Me, you will enjoy freedom; without Me, your soul remains captive and will fall in the snares of the evil one who will imprison you; so look at no one else, My love, but at your God, thrice Holy; delight in no one else on

17

earth but in Me who suckles you from His Sources with Life; pine away with love for no one on earth except for the King of kings, the First and the Last and for His House; and you, Vasiliki, on whom I posed Myself * and who hugged Me ever so tenderly and with so much affection on your cheek as a token of love, exclaiming: " I found Him whom

* Vision of 29.1.89. The Holy Spirit came as a Dove in that vision. He flew over many people who were stretching their hands, but decided to fly over to me and posed Himself on my outstretched hands, on my fingers. Then I hugged Him on my cheek.

18

my heart loves!" and you clasped Me and
held Me fast against your cheek, nor
would you let Me go, but I too had
found My bed of spices, bands sweetly
scented; "I shall give you the gift
of My Love", I said; then like drops of
pure myrrh, My words dropped in your
ear, opening it to be able to hear My
desires; "I am your Life; let yourself
be directed by grace, from now on by
Me; let your lips be as the lilies*,

*It means: let your sayings be pure.

19

distilling pure myrrh; do not give up the struggle, I will be with you; bear the Cross of Christ and be enamoured of It and I will be with you; put your faith in God and glorify the Father's Name; encourage your generation to get to know the Father; tell them that He is a gentle Father and a God of consolation; spread the Knowledge of Himself and I will be with you; tell this generation that the Amen's Name fills all the universe with a most sublime

20

perfume, a most delicate fragrance; be like a gazelle and be swift going over ravines, crossing valleys with Our Word; and I will be with you; be as a lily, through your purity of intentions, distilling pure myrrh on the Church that Christ bought with His Own Blood; let Us say one day: how fragrant your perfume, more fragrant than all the other spices and I will be with you and will keep on breathing over you, My garden, to spread your sweet perfume

21

all around; be planted in Me and grow strong in your faith with the strength of My Power, so that you will grasp the breadth and the length, the height and the depth, until you will reach to know the Love of the Son, which is beyond all knowledge, and will be filled with utter fullness of God;" this is what I said to you....

and now, My bride, espoused and clothed with Christ, adorned with My ineffable Light and inbedded like a

22

royal gem in Me, <u>take heart</u>, I am
with you, your true Companion; fragile
bride of the Most High and Father of
all and who is Bridegroom to all, guard
your thoughts on His Sovereignity and His
Splendour and feed yourself directly from
His Mouth by placing your mouth on His,
to obtain the grandeur of His Word;
the flow of His Word is sweeter than
nectar; be cleaved to your Bridegroom's Bosom and you will shine in
the world like a bright star

23

because you will be offering the world
the Word of Life; your race, My beloved, is not over, but I am with you;
although there will still be burning arrows
aimed at you because you have received
the Word of God from Me; be bold, for
I am your Armour; keep spreading your
sweet fragrance extending it in every nation,
without forgetting that I am your sweet
Lover, the Lord God, and that you,
whom I created for this purpose, are My
bride who belongs now to My Imperial

24

Household; I am the revelation* of the Son
and the Son is the revelation of the Father;
and in Our perfect wisdom We have bestow-
ed upon this generation and for the future
generations, various favours like never
       before in history; for their salvation
I raised prophets to help them understand
and reach the fullest knowledge of Our
Divine Will; I have given you to them
entirely to admonish them through this
Canticle*² and help them understand and know

* It could be underst od as " Image " too.
*² God means, His Message of " True Life in God "

25

Us and enter in the way of salvation
where the plenitude of all graces is hidden;
all the saints and angels declare now
with one melodious voice :

" we thank you O most Holy and
Adorable Trinity, Eternal Wisdom,
for supplying, in an ineffable abyss of
generosity, the whole world with
Your Canticle of Hope and Love; written
so that it will lead many to Eternal
Salvation; with exceptional grace,
You have laid out a way, scented

26

by a sweet odour of Your perfume, and
spread with sapphires, for every one to
follow and find their lovliest rest
in Eternity; and in Your divine gentleness You have found this remedy to heal
this generation;

O Spring of the universe,
Most lovable Trinity,
altogether adorable Bridegroom,
You visited once more the earth,
to speak to Your children heart
to heart, pouring on them a

27

stream of graces with anointed and
luminous knowledge of Yourself;
You, Luminous Godhead, have
anticipated this Feast* long before Your
creation; the day when, favouring
your beloved, You would call Your
creation, from the lowest to the highest,
to a day of espousals with Your Divinity,
where in those days of festivity You would
share with them a more intimate
union, imbedded like a royal gem in
You, and where You would converse

* The gift of this revelation: 'True Life in God.'

28

with them in the interiour of their
heart; in the tenderness of Your Heart
You had foreseen that this divine
union would be only sweetness, because
You would be spending Your time
with them, sharing their lives while still
on earth as You share Your splendour
with Your angels, may praise and thanks
be given to the adorable Trinity for
irrigating His flower beds*, and for
sending His light far and wide;
we give thanks to You, God,

* it means: our souls

29

as we recount Your marvels; in order to reach the abyss of human frailty, You left Your Throne and laid aside Your royal Crown*, to ornament Your creation with an overflow of Your divine Love; then, inebriated with Your Love for them, You gave Your Holy Spirit who would draw them into Your nuptial chamber*² and on Your matrimonial bed*³, spon-

*¹ expression which means : God came down to reach the level of His weak people.
*² Intimacy *³ Divine union in the Love of God.

30

taneously, uniting themselves to You;

O Holy Trinity, Treasure of the
saints and of the angels; once Your creation would be exalted with Divine Love,
they would cry out to You: " Kyrie eleisson,
Kyrie eleisson ... " while You
would be whispering in their ear :
" because you embraced impassibility, you
found a spiritual vivification in
My embrace; "

Giver of Life and Dispensor
of inestimable gifts, You have,

31

in Your tenderness, summoned the
poor as well as the rich to gather
around Your Kingly table, offering an
imperial Banquet; glory be to
the Most High, Source of ineffable
delights, Fountain that makes the
gardens fertile*, Well of Living Water,
Streams of faithful Love flowing
from Your Heart, Lover of
mankind, Bridegroom of Your creation,
we adore You and praise Your

* gardens fertile means: 'souls who progress spi-
ritualy'

32

Holy Name Thrice Holy ; amen ; "
yes, Vassula; all heaven rejoices since in
Our gracious condescension We took pity
on this generation; Christ had said: "if anyone loves Me, he will keep My Word,
and My Father will love him; and We
will come to him and make Our abode
with him;" *¹ and so We will ....

O happy seed *²! were you to be
sown in Me, your harvest will be
Paradise; were you to grow in Me,

* ¹ Jn 14:23   * ² we are God's seed

33

you would blossom and your spring flowers, since they would blossom in Spring Himself, will perfume the earth, and the earth, revived by your aromatic fragrance, will utter its first word :   " Father ! "   and it will be saved ;

You have won for Yourself this rebellious heart of mine ; in Your lavish affection and in Your Love, You have clasped my filthy hands into Yours drawing me close to You and in You, breathing a new life in my soul ; and with a baptisimal kiss You ended my rebellion ; O indis-cribable delight of my soul, You visited me not daring to show me, in the beginning,

34

the immensity of Your Love, lest my heart would
be too small to contain it; You abstained
from revealing to me entirely the ardour of
Your Love lest I would run away in
my human frailty; but then, in the
exuberance of Your Love,
You wedded me ....
You wedded me, despite my great
wretchedness and guilt, wholly uniting me
to Your Triune Holiness; this free
gift given by Your Own Will, given
to an unworthy worm as myself,
baffles me still to this day ....

O Sunshine of my soul; You who
so delicately fed me on curds and honey*
here You are now, visiting the
earth once more; but the earth again
mistrusts You and refuses to welcome You;

* Symbolic description of 'curds and honey' is in
this context: purity, gentleness and tenderness.

35

My Beloved went down to His garden*[1]
to the bed of spices,*[2]
to pasture His flock*[3] in the gardens,
and gather lilies;*[4]

My Beloved came to call His Own Flock,
and gather lilies in the fields who have
no other care but to LOVE; He came
to gather His lilies for His Own
good pleasure;

Divine Wisdom visited the earth to
remind His Own that there is but one
theology, that of contemplating You
in Your Triune Glory;

*[1] The earth
*[2] Souls
*[3] To feed us spiritually
*[4] and turn us like the lilies; make us pure.

36

So let me be Your rose without thorns, most delicate Bridegroom, and you, my Living Water; there, my stem placed in this Living Water, will not die, but will draw life and will live eternally since I will be plunged in the Eternal God Himself.

You have been favoured by the odor of My fragrance*¹, and I allowed you to contemplate My Holy Face which shone on you; *² no, this memory of My Holy Face will never dissipate from your memory; I transcend earth and

¹* His Holy Presence
²* Immediately the vision of His Divine Face came up in the surface of my memory It remains in my body only because of the Holy Spirit's divine power.

37

heaven in majesty and splendour and
My Name and no other is sublime,
raising the poor in spirit to join Me;
I move in them and they move in Me;
I have, out of My exuberant Love, as
I have inspired you to call it, offered
you free gifts in abundance, for I am
only interested in those who fear Me*
and in those who rely on My Love; no,
I have not come to inflict punishment
on you, but instead, I came to you

* Ps 147 : 11

38

to wed you, and as a bridegroom who
lavishes his bride with gifts, I adorned you with My divine gifts; it is not
by the eloquence of words I am moved
or affected, but by a contrite spirit; does
not Scripture teach you to love virtue?
were you to seek Me in simplicity of heart,
not putting Me to the test, then I, in
My Benevolence will come down from heaven
as a lightning inside your body and be
your lamp; you have been taught that
the lamp of your body is your eye,

39

and so it is, because a diseased eye has
no vision and has only darkness, whereas
a healthy eye illuminates the view; I am
this lamp and anyone who has Me within
him, will seek the true virtues and not
the vices. I am the real lamp of your
body that fills your whole body with the
treasures and splendours of Our Kingdom; these treasures and splendours are
the virtues; where there is Light there is
virtue; where there is Darkness there is vice;
do not be mistaken and cling to this dying

40

world, but be faithful to Me and you will live with Me in love; love virtue; in the beginning, Vassula, you were asked to live holy and be holy; I had also counselled you that were you to strike deep roots in Me, you would not sway in the wind nor would any of your branches snap off with any kind of tempest; then your fruit would be plenty, enough to feed a multitude and generations; were you to remain loyal to Us, I said I would grant you special favours, and so I did;

41

I imbedded you like a royal gem in Me,
and addressed you; I refreshed you and nourished you to grow in virtue; I gave you such
virtues as love and patience, wisdom, knowledge,
fortitude and perseverance; Christ had
offered you His patience and at the same
time, the grace of hope; to build your
hope that one day holiness would be rewarded I have taught you to endure all the
tests put to you with a holy patience; you
sought, in your human frailty to please Us;
so We bent over you and loved you;

42

Wisdom is given to mere children and so We, in Our Triune Holiness, found simplicity of heart and instructed you that you had to <u>acquire</u> Wisdom, but We would be helping you; We said that We would help you imitate Us and be Our living altar upon which We would place Our knowledge, so that you would understand and know Us; you sought to please Us, and We found Our comfort in you; I am the Spirit who teaches and gives temperance; soul, let your sparks die down even more; your closeness to Us is wealth for your soul;

43

yes, your closeness to Our royal Munificence
renders you perseverant not only for your
mission but to reach an invincible Holiness,
I said to you, My beloved, to love virtue, and
I compared you to a tree which has many
branches, rich in foliage, because you were rooted
in Me, the Source of Love, and from that
Source you were   irrigated to produce
many and a variety of fruits, fruits
of virtues; I say a variety of virtues
because any one who is rooted in Love
which is the principle of all virtues,

44

will give birth to all other virtues; does
not Scripture say: "Love endures, Love
is always patient and kind; Love is never
jealous or boastful; Love is not proud; it
is not rude or selfish; Love does not
take offence and holds no rancour; Love
takes no pleasure in other people's sins or
vices, but rejoices in the Holy Spirit
and delights in the truth; it is always
ready to excuse, to trust, to hope and
to endure whatever comes;" I have given
you the virtue of fortitude to be the

45

principle of all your other virtues in you;
since I was preparing your soul for this
battle of your times, where good is deformed
into evil; in the beginning, Christ instructed
you as well as the Father, through Me,
that We would be sending you; My loved
one, in the vile depths of sin, where iniquity and vice are worn like a crown on those
who recrucify Christ; We showed you,
through visions infused into your intellect,
that We would be sending you in the
nest of vipers, and so with the virtue of

46

trust in Us; together with the virtue of
fortitude, you would endure and persevere;
you endured all the injustices, the venomous
arrows thrust on you, with this virtue;
you endured great trials for the sake of
Our Name; and many who contradicted
you were not able to break you;
although from the exterior you appeared
frail, I rendered you strong from within,
proof that I am well within you, and
that your virtue is indeed rooted in
the Truth; as I have said, if you are

47

rooted in Me, who am the Source of Divine
Love, you will obtain the virtue of love,
then like little branches, Love will give
birth to other virtues; there are numerous
virtues given to each one, who, by grace
were raised to love Me; and everything
that is distributed is distributed by Me;
We once said to you in the beginning that
you would have no rest and that at
times your grief would be intolerable at
seeing the deafness and stubborness of
certain souls, but by your suffering for

48

Our sake, you have proved your patience, which is as I have told you linked to the Source, which is love; to widen the space of My Dwelling place*, I removed all that was obstructing Me, and My light rose in the darkness and the shadows became like noon; I gave strength to your bones and I flowered you with My Presence; be strong and prove your- self worthy as My bride, wedded to the Truth; be perseverant and strong

* my soul

49

with My Spirit of fortitude, to continue to bear witness to the Truth with zeal and courage; with this virtue that I give by My Grace to martyrs, you can overcome all your detractors and all those who never cease hailing the death of My angel*; like the sun you will continue shining in Our Triune Presence and in every nation We send you; you seek to please Us by enduring the pains of lengthy journeys to enliven the

* I knew that the Holy Spirit meant me.

50

Church and defend it; anyone who defends
faithfully the Church and witnesses are, for Us,
like living torches because their words flare
in the darkness of the world; I give
them a warrior's heart, to fight the
good fight of faith and justice and join
in this spiritual battle of your times
My archangels Michael and Raphael, who
are predominant in strength and valiant
Warriors of Justice, observing through My
Light every aspect of human behaviour....
you sought to please Us, with

51

devout affection and loyalty, so We hid
you in the shadow of Our Hand, taking
you in Our care; Mediator of every one,
I Am; Guarantor of your well-being,
I Am; sublime Source of Unity of
the Christians I Am; supreme Unity of
the Father and the Son, I Am;
Unction to the poor in spirit, I Am;
Unceasing Prayer within you, I Am;
Bridegroom to you all and Perpetual
Companion, I Am; beloved bride, you
have now learnt from My Mouth, and

52

through grace in an ineffable manner,
what concerns Us; I have been teaching
you that knowledge of God, through
Me, is trinitarian knowledge to
refute heresies and the like; ah, Vassula!
the One whom you allowed to take
root in your inmost being is the Truth
who transfigures souls into a delightful
Paradise where a variety of trees can
be found which represent all sorts of
virtues; these are the heavens in which
We dwell perpetually;   and now

53

I have sung to you as a bridegroom would sing to his bride: a canticle of love; a canticle of divine love to remind all of you that you are heirs to Our Kingdom; this was hymned to you by the Hymn* Himself, to allow you all to taste, while still on earth, My supreme sweetness eternally joined to you; so the Bridegroom welcomes you by say-ing: 'come now, with a contrite spirit and have your fill in Me; let all

* God's words are like a hymn and God is heard as a hymn.

54

who are thirsty come! I have the Water
of Life and I have it for free; I, the
Lover of mankind, the Lord God, ask
you, daughter of the Trinity, to take the
other two Canticles, hymned to you by
the Father and the Son, together with
this one and name Our Work:

Canticle of the Bridegroom;

in Our Divine Canticle are many sayings
of Our Triune sweetness, with amorous
teachings so that many trees would
prosper and grow; but as for the barren

55

trees, I shall come, with a host of
angels and uproot them in winter and
so will be twice dead; inscribe on your
heart, all of you, this fundamental truth:
"the Lord God knows those who are
His Own and so allows them to come
near Him," these are destined to attain
perfection in the divine and intimate
union with Us; they are called to be
transfigured in Us and be one with Us;
their old self will be no more, but in
an ineffable manner I gave always to My

56

saints, I would deify them in Our union; through Me, I deify all those to whom I am united and they no longer speak with their own mind but in the manner I would speak; they no longer see with their eyes but in the manner I would see things; their acts would be My acts; a golden ring was given to you,* an ornament of finest gold, the day of your spiritual espousals, as a symbol of¹: sharing the Cross; therefore, I invite you once more to endure with

* Vision of 23.3.87. Christ offering me a wedding ring.

57

patience your trials; grant Us your time,
and now, beloved daughter, come and
rest in Us;

Let us seek the understanding of the
invisible God by simplicity and purity
of heart;

Let us seek the understanding of His
exuberant Love in the divine union
and intimacy that His Majesty has deigned
to offer us, by wholly abandoning ourselves
to Him;

In Your great condescendance You have,
Lover of all mankind, hymned to us
to rejoice us; You have, as a bridegroom who prepares for his bride a
banquet, You have prepared for all
of us a royal banquet so that we
can all feast on the bounty

58

of Your house; You give us drink
from Your river of pleasure; yes,
for with You, my Lord, is the
fountain of Life, by Your Light
we see the Light;

As a doe longs for running streams,
   so longs my soul for You, my God;
my soul thirsts for God,
      the God of Life;
      the God of Hope;
      the God of Consolation;
when shall I go to see the face
   of God again?

My heart had said of You:
      " seek His Holy Countenance;"
and, as a king would pay tribute
   to his queen,   in this same manner,
in Your perfect goodness, You paid
   tribute to my most unworthy soul
      by showing Your beauty, by
      showing me Your Holy Face;

59

Saving Fortress of my soul,
            shepherd me;
and let my soul enjoy Your sweetness;
You have given strength to feeble hands
schooling me by addressing me in a
most delightful way, shining Your Light
on murk and deep shadow;

Down there, in the murk, Your Majesty
descended with sorrow in Your Eyes,
to free the slave-of-the-murky-world,
            and reach my tomb.

I had died for lack of Wisdom.

Who was I, my Beloved, to make so
much of me? Was it right for You,
My King, to fix Your Eyes on me and
    adorn my soul in royal vestments
with Your Word, without risking to
    cheapen Your Works for my sake?

60

Yes, I had perished as I was
leaving the womb; like a still-born child
I came into the world with a cloud
hanging over me; I thought
I was, but I had never been, not
until You came to blow life in
me;

When I opened my eyes and saw from
a distance Your Presence, my heart
blossomed like a flower and all
that was like crumbling rotten wood
within me transmogrified into a
garden; then my cheeks filled with
happy laughter to see my Redeemer
standing so near me; and my lips
broke a cry of joy from the moment
I drew the breath of Life.

Your Works, Emmanuel, are great,
beyond all reckoning,
Your Marvels, Emmanuel, past all
counting; and now, I will

61

give free rein to my joy; I shall
let my delighted soul speak out:

Today I need not call the tomb I layed in:
                    " my bridegroom" and to the
worm : " my friend, brother and sister;"

Today I call Life : " my Bridegroom,
      my friend, brother and sister"; in
You, I gather my myrrh, from You
I am nourished with honey, and wine
and milk is the drink You give me;

And so, I pray kneeling, and I entreat
   with You to gather all Your Flowers *
so that they may know that Your
   company, Holy One, is radiance
to the soul, riches not to be
numbered. Your Companionship,
   Myrrh of my soul, is pure
contentment;

* Souls

62

I am now like a child, happy
and disposed; whosoever ventures
to exhale fiery breaths against
Your child, Your strong Arm
will be there to protect it;

Evil can never triumph over love,
and where love is, You are ....

I shall never be deserted ....

do you think I am not touched,* My
beloved, with all My Heart? do
not listen to all the noise they make
around you; cloistered in your
Saviour's Heart you are; in there
is your refreshment; remain in Me,
My sister, My own; open your
* Jesus spoke

63

hand ; ... having recognized your unworthiness, in so doing, you
have offered Me a bouquet of flowers,
and your abandonment; you have recognized that I, who am the Way
the Truth and the Life, came to your
tomb and resurrected you; and all
the graces and gifts I have given

* Jesus leaned His beautiful Head and graciously Kissed the interiour of my right hand. then
placed it on His cheek, manifesting His
tenderness and love; then drawing it
down again, He made the sign of the
cross inside it, on my palm.

64

you, were given to an unmerited soul;
yield to what is good, and you
will end up with honour in
front of My Throne; winnow good
from evil; ecclesia will revive,
My beloved one; I bless you;
I am with you;

A ☧ Ω